CHILDREN IN CRISIS:

A NEW COMMITMENT

CHILDREN IN CRISIS:

A NEW COMMITMENT

Phyllis Kilbourn, editor

121 East Huntington Drive, Monrovia, California 91016-3400 USA

CHILDREN IN CRISIS: A NEW COMMITMENT

Phyllis Kilbourn, editor

ISBN 0-912552-97-2

Published by MARC, a division of World Vision International, 121 E. Huntington Drive, Monrovia, California 91016-3400, U.S.A.

Printed in the United States of America. Interior page layout: Marjorie McDermid. Cover art and design: Diane Ulmer Pedersen. Cover production: Richard Sears.

All Scripture quotations, unless otherwise indicated, are taken from the HOLY BIBLE, NEW INTERNATIONAL VERSION®. Copyright © 1973, 1978, 1984 by International Bible Society. Used by permission of Zondervan Publishing House. All rights reserved.

The poem "Prayer for Children" is from the book *Gold Cord* by Amy Carmichael, and is used by permission of the publisher, Christian Literature Crusade.

The Scripture quotation in chapter 8 is from *The Message*, copyright © 1993, 1994, 1995. Used by permission of NavPress Publishing Group.

Prayer for Children

Father, hear us, we are praying,
Hear the words our hearts are saying,
We are praying for our children.

Keep them from the powers of evil,
From the secret, hidden peril,
Father, hear us for our children.

From the whirlpool that would suck them,
From the treacherous quicksand, pluck them,
Father, hear us for our children.

From the worldling's hollow gladness,
From the sting of faithless sadness,
Father, Father, keep our children.

Through life's troubled waters steer them,
Through life's bitter battles cheer them,
Father, Father, be Thou near them.

Read the language of our longing,
Read the wordless pleadings thronging,
Holy Father, for our children.

And wherever they may bide,
Lead them home at eventide.

—Amy Carmichael

Also by Phyllis Kilbourn:

Healing the Children of War

Contents

Part 2
A Biblical Response

Part 3
Strategies and Opportunities

Part 4
Equipping for Ministry

Part 5
Concluding Reflections

Part 6
Appendix

Contributing Authors

Neil T. Anderson. Ed.D. from Pepperdine University, M.Div. and D. Min. from Talbot School of Theology. Founder and president of Freedom In Christ Ministries. Taught for ten years at Talbot School of Theology; author of eleven books, including *The Bondage Breaker* and *The Seduction of Our Children*.

Elnora Avarientos. Diploma in Social Work from the University of the Philippines. Community development worker with Foster Parents Plan, the National Womens Christian Association and the Philippines' Department of Social Welfare and Development. Now World Vision International's Director for Ministry Support.

Jan Bell. Founder, in 1987, of Kids Can Make a Difference—a program to integrate a missions perspective into any curriculum. Author, mentor, workshop leader and director of leadership and ministry development for Christ's American Baptist Church, Spring Grove, Pennsylvania.

Edward T. Bradley. Founder and president of Oakseed Ministries International. Served on staff with the International Fellowship of Evangelical Students in Pakistan and InterVarsity Christian Fellowship. A church planter, he is an ordained pastor in the Presbyterian Church of America.

Howard E. Brant. D. Min. from Trinity International University, Deerfield, Illinois. Missionary with SIM for 23 years, now acting Deputy General Director (1995) with special responsibilities for Asia and the South Pacific. Conference ministry, preaching and teaching the Scripture in cross-cultural settings.

Dan Brewster. Doctorate in Missiology from Fuller School of World Mission. Compassion International's director for program development. Involved in child and family development ministries for 18 years, mostly overseas. Visited or supervised child and family development or relief projects in more than 50 countries.

Andy Butcher. A professional journalist for 21 years. Joined Youth With A Mission in 1989, where he directs the international communication office's Press & Media Services department. His book, *Street Children: The Tragedy and Challenge of the World's Millions of Modern-day Oliver Twists*, published by Nelson-WORD (UK, 1996).

Perry Downs. Ph.D. from New York University. Professor of Christian education and director of the doctor of education program at Trinity International University, Deerfield, Illinois. Author of *Teaching for Spiritual Growth* (Zondervan, 1994). As licensed foster parents, Dr. Downs and his wife have cared for 28 children in difficult circumstances.

Warren Heard. M.Div., M.A. in counseling and Th.M. from Trinity International University, Deerfield, Illinois; Ph.D. in New Testament from University of Aberdeen, Scotland; Ed. D. candidate at Northern Illinois University in Counseling. Professor of New Testament and Psychology and Counseling at Trinity International University.

Peter J. Hohmann. M.Ed. and M.C. (Master of Counseling) Arizona State University, Associate Pastor (Missions and Christian Education), Mechanicsville Christian Center, Mechanicsville, Virginia. Vice-president of the board for Kids Can Make A Difference. Led 18 missions projects to Latin America and Asia and conducted workshops on involving children in missions.

Esther Ilnisky. Founder of Esther Network International: Children's Global Prayer Movement, networking with the

AD2000 and Beyond Movement in the united prayer track and children's sub-track. Conducts global intercessory prayer gatherings and prayer workshops to train children, parents and mentors in global prayer.

Phyllis Kilbourn. Ed.D. from Trinity International University, Deerfield, Illinois. Missionary with WEC International since 1967, serving in Kenya and Liberia. Edited *Healing the Children of War*, a handbook for ministry to children who have suffered deep traumas, (MARC 1995) and a handbook for ministry to street children to be published also by MARC (1997).

Sandra Levinson. Vice-president of the Alliance for Children Everywhere. Responsible for community outreach, fund raising and mobilization of churches and individuals on behalf of children. Left the corporate business world to minister to suffering children.

Samuel R. Martin. D.Min., graduate of the Universities of Manchester and Edinburgh. Senior pastor of Bayfair Baptist Church, Pickering, Ontario, Canada. Founder and president of The Arms of Jesus Children's Mission, Inc. Served on the boards of Trans World Radio and Christian Blind Mission. Has led ten short-term mission teams and visited numerous mission fields.

Marjorie McDermid. Graduate of the Full Gospel Bible Institute, Eston, Saskatchewan, Canada. Missionary to Equatorial Guinea, West Africa with WEC International. Has worked in various children's ministries. Twenty years editor of *WORLDWIDE THRUST*, WEC's bimonthly communiqué in U.S.A.

Randy Miller. M.A in Communications, California State University, Fullerton. Managing Editor of *TOGETHER*, a quarterly journal published by World Vision. Traveled extensively throughout the world, mostly on assignment for World Vision. Articles and photographs published internationally.

Timothy Monsma. Ph.D. from Fuller Theological Seminary, Pasadena, California. Taught mission and missionary anthropology at Reformed Bible College in Grand Rapids and at Mid-America Reformed Seminary, Iowa. Served as a missionary in Nigeria for 12 years. Currently Africa Director of Action International Ministries based in Bothell, Washington.

Karen Moran. Coordinator for the Children's Global Prayer Movement of Esther Network International, West Palm Beach, Florida, a program to mobilize, train and equip children worldwide to pray effectively for their generation.

Diane Ulmer Pedersen (cover). B.F.A. in Fine Arts from Denison University. Studied advertising and illustration at Moore College of Art, Philadelphia, Pennsylvania. Free-lance painter and graphic designer, she was art director/designer for WEC International for several years. Her work as a folk artist has appeared in *Colonial Homes* and *Woman's Day* magazines as well as in *Early American Life*'s directory of the 200 best traditional craftsmen.

Alison Rader. An HIV/AIDS program consultant working with the Salvation Army through the international office in London. She is an experienced community development person with wide international experience in facilitation of program design and participatory evaluation.

Larry W. Sharp. Ph.D. in comparative education from the University of Calgary, Alberta, Canada; M.A. in Education from Azusa Pacific University. Director for U.S.A. of UFM International since 1993. Missionary to Brazil with UFM as teacher and principal of Amazon Valley Academy for 15 years and as Brazil field director for eight years.

Edward T. Welch. Ph.D. in neuropsychology from the University of Utah, Salt Lake City, Utah; M. Div. in biblical studies from Biblical Theological Seminary, Hatfield, Pennsylvania. Licensed psychologist, director of counseling at The Christian Counseling & Educational Foundation, Laverock, Pennsylvania and faculty member at Westminster Theological Seminary, Philadelphia, Pennsylvania. Author of *The Counselor's Guide to the Brain and Its Disorders, Addictive Behavior.*

Bill Wilson. Graduate of Southeastern Bible College, Lakeland, Florida. Appointed by President Bush to the National Commission on America's Urban Families. Pastor of Metro Ministries in the Bushwick/Bedford-Stuyvesant area of Brooklyn, New York which was honored by *Guideposts* magazine as Church of the Year in 1990.

Jennie Woods. President of Alliance for Children Everywhere, she has been a missionary to children for nearly 30 years. Was responsible for the establishment of an emergency crisis care home for children in Guatemala and later in Peru. Speaks and writes to encourage Christians to become involved in ministry to the world's children.

Acknowledgements

I am deeply grateful for the outstanding team of writers the Lord assembled to contribute to the urgent message of this book. Each writer carries a special burden for the world's suffering children and each has truly conveyed the heartbeat and longing of God for our "smallest members" who are so precious in his sight. The authors have given their time and expertise freely as a gift with the expectation that children in difficult circumstances will be the recipients of much blessing and hope through the fruits of this book.

A jeweler spends countless hours cutting and polishing gems of great worth, seeking to bring out the stones' very best qualities. The Lord provided me with a superb "support team" to help in the polishing and refining work of the manuscripts the authors so carefully crafted. This team willingly gave their gifts and skills because they believe in the immense worth of the message this book contains. Many prayer supporters, including our WEC retirees, laid a foundation of prayer and encouragement which undergirded this process through to completion.

I must first acknowledge the tremendous debt of gratitude I owe to Marjorie McDermid, for twenty years editor of *Worldwide Thrust*, WEC's bimonthly communiqué. How timely that the Lord led her to lay down her *Thrust* pen just in time to assume the roles of copy editor and layout designer for this book! Marjorie even assumed the role of author for one chapter. I value the many gifts and skills Marjorie has contributed to this book—skillfully polishing the gems far beyond my abilities. I have also cherished her prayer support and constant encouragement during the many pressure–filled weeks this project entailed.

Other "diamond polishers" include Grace Palmer who labored long at the tedious task of entering corrections and offered helpful suggestions; George and Marie Poos and Ed Stuebner whose labor of love resulted in the attractively designed Tool Box in Appendix A; Mary Ellen (Machamer) Longo who kept writers and editors connected through a continous flow of faxes around the globe and WEC colleagues Nancy Land, Joanne Major, Elwin Palmer and Judy Raymo who contributed much time to read and critique manuscripts.

A diamond's beauty commences with an outward shine that penetrates to its very core. Diane Ulmer Pedersen, special friend and former WEC colleague, provided the outer beauty of the book through her sensitively rendered cover art design and layout.

The highest reward we could desire for our labors is to witness the beauty of children's faces lit up by the joy of restored hope, happiness, laughter, dignity and a sense of self–worth.

Phyllis Kilbourn

Foreword

Children. They are the ultimate silent majority. Though they make up nearly half of the human family, they bear far more than their share of the world's miseries. Society's ills spiral downward and inflict their cruelest blows on our vulnerable little ones. When adults get hungry, children starve. When adults get sick, children die. In the last decade more *children* have died in our global battles than *soldiers*. Every day, 35,000 of these precious young lives are snuffed out by *preventable causes* because we lack the heart and courage to fight on their behalf. *Every day!* Without influence, power or options, they suffer silently, their tears and fears known only to God.

You hold in your hands a truly remarkable book. Phyllis Kilbourn has given voice to unsung heroes among us. So rarely are such powerful issues presented and so seldom are such humble visionaries heard that you may not recognize a single author among them. Those of us who have given our lives to the cause of children no longer find this surprising—we scarcely know each other. Children don't bestow awards, honorary degrees or shining trophies. They can bestow only hugs and kisses, their eyes shining with gratitude and hope. But for the children's champions whose words are about to stir your heart, these are reward enough.

D.L. Moody, the great evangelist, viewed children the way we do at Compassion International, and the way you will at the end of this book. As he was climbing into bed one night after an evangelistic crusade, his wife asked, "Well, Honey, how did it go?"

Moody replied, "Great! Two and a half converts!"

"Oh, how old was the child?" his wife inquired. "Oh, no," he corrected her. "Two children and one adult! The children have their whole lives before them: the adult's life is half gone."

To my dismay, I find such perception rare among Christian leadership today. I recently attended a conference of mission executives to discuss strategy for reaching our world for Christ by the turn of the century. Strongly supportive of this powerful commitment, I came—note pad in hand—to glean tactical insight for Compassion's ministry. In two days of presentations from world leaders in evangelism, I heard the words "child" or "children" only 12 times and never in relation to a strategic thrust. Yet, missiologists inform us that 85 percent of people who give their lives to Christ do so between the ages of 4 and 14. The omission of children's ministry from this massive effort, therefore, was—to say the least—staggering irony. I wanted to jump up and shout, "People, close your eyes for a moment and picture this sea of humanity stretched across our world. If every other person in that mental image is not a child, you don't understand who you are trying to reach. Here we have half of the world ripe for harvesting, and you don't even have them targeted in your programs!" The amazing fact is that of all the money given to missions less than 15 percent is spent on children.

Currently great emphasis focuses evangelistic efforts on the people in the 10/40 window. I grew up in the 10/40 window. Much of Compassion's ministry takes place within the 10/40 window, and I pray daily for the 10/40 window. Yet, as much as missions zero in on this important part of the world, they have overlooked the obvious window within a window. At Compassion we call this target the 4/14 window. These children are open and receptive to the gospel, but because in our adult-focused zeal we view them as "just children," they are forgotten.

This fact should not surprise us: even Jesus' disciples considered children too unimportant to disturb the great Master's teaching. Straining in their mothers' arms, slipping through the disciples' legs, the "least of these" struggled to run into the arms of this kind and gentle man. They knew from the twinkle in his eye, the smile embedded in the lines of his weather-beaten face and the warmth of his voice that if they could just get to him, they would be welcomed into his loving embrace. His admonition rings through the ages and chastises us still: *Let the children come to me.*

May this book inform you, inspire you and equip you to reach out to the children—the children in your life and the children across the world—for Christ and his kingdom.

Wesley Stafford
President, Compassion International

Introduction

Phyllis Kilbourn

This book calls attention to the "forgotten" of the world's children. In spite of the fact that they are the most vulnerable, often children are societies' most neglected, abandoned and abused members. This book doesn't simply paint pictures of the desperate situations of these children and record their sobs. It also demands a biblical, God-directed response from every reader.

Part One contrasts the happy, carefree childhood God intended children to enjoy with the appalling realities of the abusive circumstances countless millions are forced to endure as a result of war, HIV/AIDS, forced child labor, living on danger-filled city streets, being sold into a life of prostitution or simply being born a girl child. The contrast also portrays the immensity of the children's loss in these abusive environments.

Sadly, because of the immensity of the task, the authors were unable to include all the abusive circumstances children confront. Millions more are beaten, battered, kidnapped, sexually abused and devalued in innumerable ways by individuals in their homes and communities. How incredible that children, Yahweh's best gift, should have to endure such horrifying abuse! The problem is so invasive in the world's societies that the final descriptive word on the circumstances of these children could never be written.

Part Two addresses the crucial issue of the church's response to the children's plight. The authors in this section force church and mission leaders, and individuals, to examine their commitment to ministry with children in light of Scripture. Only a strong biblical response from each member of the body of Christ to care for these, our most defenseless members, will suffice.

Part Three and Part Four enable us to make concrete our biblical response of ministry to these precious children. Part Three provides strategies and opportunities to utilize in reaching out to them whether they are in faraway Africa or right on our back doorstep, including the inner city. Some chapters focus on the exciting ways God is using children in fulfilling the Great Commission! When we rescue children from their abusive conditions, God can use them mightily in his service.

Part Four prepares us for outreach to children by providing some basic tools to use in ministry; ministry that restores God's design to lost childhoods. You will be equipped with basic counseling skills and techniques, an understanding of the role of Christian nurture in holistic intervention planning and a biblical understanding of the issues involved in ministry to the world's suffering children.

In Part Five, Larry Sharp breathes hope into the children's overwhelming situations by illustrating what can be accomplished when individuals, churches and missions jointly rise to the challenge of making a biblical commitment of ministry to children in crisis. He also presents strong reasons why such a commitment is worth any sacrifice.

As you enter the children's world through the pages of this book, our prayer is that you will experience God enlarging your vision, burdening your heart and generating a God-given compassion toward these children. As this process takes place, prayerfully consider what specific commitment God would have you make to his special treasures, those so often despised and devalued by the world but so precious to the Father.

(And, don't forget to check the Tool Box in Appendix A! It contains a generous sampling of resources available to get you "up and running.")

Part 1

Childhood in Crisis

1
Contrasting Images of Childhood

Phyllis Kilbourn

Children. They come in an assortment of shapes, sizes and colors. They have differing joys, expectations, hopes and dreams. God has uniquely designed each child in his own image—creating each one as an exciting bundle of potentiality. He also has planned the gift of childhood to be a special time for nurturing children's God-given gifts and abilities. With the help and encouragement of family, friends and extended family members, children should find childhood a time to discover the person God created them to be.

IMAGES OF A HEALTHY CHILDHOOD

Childhood, especially in times past, recalls some very happy and memorable experiences of that brief span of time in which life was left uncluttered by adult-sized upsets, problems, decision-making, choices, responsibilities and complexities. Bedtime stories predictably began, "Once upon a time" and ended, "They lived happily ever after." And as soon as you were launched into the "once upon a time," nothing was impossible; you were swept as far away as your imagination could carry you!

Such a "fairy tale" existence, however, was not always the way things were! Childhood even back then had problems and woes to be dealt with on a daily basis. But apart from family deaths and sporadic bouts of cuts, bumps, bruises and broken bones, childhood crises generally bottomed out at the level of peril experienced by my brother.

Whiling away a beautiful summer day, Gordon was sprawled under a favorite tree, his faithful pal, old Shep, beside him. He was ready to enjoy his newest story book when his eyes gazed upward to the deep blue sky filled with puffy white clouds. Gordon's mind was quickly diverted to deciphering pictures in the clouds: dogs, giants, turtles and trains belching smoke.

Suddenly, awestruck and filled with terror, Gordon ran for the safety of home. Breathlessly he cried out, "Mom, Mom, what is holding up the sky? What's keeping it from falling down on me?"

Childhood crises aside, my most vivid recollections of a carefree childhood revolve around words and images that reflect a sense of freedom: boundless energy, carefree play, infectious giggles, happy laughter, simplicity, trust, security. Such "freedom images" are portrayed in children happily romping over a grassy hill on a warm, breezy day or flying kites that effortlessly soar skyward along with the children's spirits; or blowing enchanted pipes that waft delightful multicolored bubbles high in the air, free to spiral at will.

THE BIBLICAL PATTERN FOR CHILDHOOD CARE

The Psalmist reminds us that children are a gift—an inheritance—from God (127:3). Surely God expects us to care for his "gift" with a heart of love; a love such as Paul describes in 1 Corinthians 13: 7: "It [love] always protects, . . . always hopes, always perseveres."

Love always protects

Protection and safety are foundational to a child's healthy development. Home always lies at the heart of a safe and happy childhood. No matter what woes or crises a child might experience growing up in his or her expanding world, home should always be there to serve as a safe retreat; a place where love is an unconditional given. In this safe haven, the child's daily joys and experiences can be shared freely, and child-sized heartaches are soothed and healed with love.

In healthy homes where relationships are based on love and trust, children develop a sense of self-esteem that molds their identity. Healthy relationships also provide a basis for developmental growth and spiritual integrity. In such an environment, children are equipped to discover the persons God created them to be. The encouragement offered and sense of self-worth imparted in the home produce happy children who can trust their world, their feelings and, eventually, their God.

The children, in communities that loved and cared for their children, also could depend on neighbors who were friendly, helpful and ready to protect them. These friends were ready to offer a cheery "hello," extend an invitation to come in for fresh homemade cookies and a glass of milk or allow a sneak glimpse of some adorable, newborn kittens. It was even more enriching when relationships with neighbors formed a two-way street; elderly neighbors being appreciative of children's helping hands to shovel snow, bring in the mail or carry groceries from the nearby store.

Love always hopes, always perseveres

Parents' love for their children causes them to hope the best for them. They know such hopeful expectations will require perseverance in training—a training which will prepare their children to one day become responsible adults. One way of accomplishing this training in my childhood was through the "home schooling" provided not just by household chores, but also through my parents investing time in their children. Working alongside us, our parents taught skills which they hoped would one day be used in our own homes or jobs.

In this training, the importance of responsibility and doing one's best were always stressed. When Mother sent me out to collect the eggs, she expected me to check all the nests—not quitting in a few minutes to play. When my turn to wash dishes rolled around, I was to be diligent to complete the task, not hiding the dirty pans in the oven! When helping with the laundry, I was encouraged to do my best in folding it neatly.

Along with perseverance in training, came perseverance in discipline. Although sometimes trying to parents, consistency in discipline is also a vital part of childhood training. Children everywhere are constantly tempted to evade chores and responsibilities. Discipline, however, is essential in providing children with healthy boundaries and a framework of authority. Learning obedience and respect is a lifelong task that must begin in childhood.

The church also played a vital role in preparing children for adulthood. Lessons learned from "home schooling" were reinforced in Sunday school classrooms. Teachers had the opportunity to instill in youthful hearts the wonderful truth that Jesus is a special Friend who loves and cares for them. Children were assured that Jesus would always be near to help them in their daily encounters with fears, troubles, obedience problems or with learning new skills.

Results of following God's pattern

When the biblical pattern of caring for children with a heart of love is honored, family and community leaders provide children with an abundance of loving, trust-filled relationships. These relationships give children a sense of security, identity, belonging, love and happiness. Such ingredients of childhood enable children to thrive happily and to mature according to God's intended pattern.

IMAGES OF A MARRED CHILDHOOD

Just as I have witnessed children living a carefree and joy-filled childhood, I also have witnessed firsthand many others who have had their childhood ruthlessly snatched from them. Abuse and violence toward children have become rampant around the world. Such poured-out abuse has caused millions of childhood images of joy, freedom and safety to become radically altered or altogether erased.

The United Nation's description of a normal childhood has become a hollow mockery to millions:

> The children of the world are innocent, vulnerable, and dependent. They are also curious, active, and full of hope. Their time should be one of joy and peace, of playing, learning and growing. Their future should be shaped in harmony and cooperation. Their lives should mature as they broaden their perspectives and gain new experiences.[1]

Tragically, just a glimpse of the changing images of childhood for the millions of children living in difficult circumstances reveals the depth of loss children experience when they are deprived of a normal, healthy childhood.

Why are such radical changes occurring? Because children in much of the world no longer are provided with a living environment conducive to their happiness, growth and development. They also aren't granted the protection and basic tools of childhood needed for healthy development. Experiencing happiness and fulfillment in childhood depends on whether a child's God-given potential is nurtured and developed or crushed through abuse and neglect.

Traditionally, people assumed children would be protected by adult members of society. What an indictment on many societies, including American, that children as young as three years of age must now be taught to protect themselves from perpetrators of the violence and abuse that have become a part of daily life in their homes and neighborhoods! And who would imagine that in many so-called "modern" societies it has become necessary to form anti-slavery societies to rescue young children from harmful exploitation?

Our children are being forced to learn two extremely painful, sad and tragic lessons: the world is no longer a safe place in which to live, and adults cannot always be trusted.

On a recent newscast, violinist Isaac Stern expressed what he considers a basic right for all children: "Every child has the right to know there's beauty in the world." But how is a child to find beauty when the sights and sounds of his or her world include:

- racial violence resulting in random murders
- exploding bombs and burned out villages
- mutilated bodies scattered everywhere
- wailing air raid sirens
- abject conditions of poverty in the ghettos
- smelly, rat-infested city dumps as the source of today's food—perhaps even as the place called "home"
- slovenly-kept brothel "prisons"
- dust-choked rock quarries where children chip rocks up to twelve hours a day
- almost total confinement to a small, dark hut because a care giver fears caring for a child victim of AIDS . . . .

One could paint endless bleak landscapes containing little, if any, beauty. No wonder children have forgotten how to laugh and play!

11

RESULTS OF A MARRED CHILDHOOD

When children live in traumatic situations, their hope is replaced by despair. Their infectious giggles, happy laughter and the joy of receiving parental love and nurture, which make their spirits carefree, are replaced with paralyzing fear, mistrust and deep grief. They carry burdens and responsibilities far too heavy for any child to bear. Deep in their spirits an overwhelming sense of hopelessness springs up; they see no opportunities to develop their God-given potential.

The new "roles" also rob children of their happy laughter. In war, for example, children often are forced to "grow up quickly" and assume parental care for siblings or "turn men overnight" and be trained in the art of killing and destruction. Poverty in the ghettos has forced thousands of children to give up both play and school to somehow help eke out a livelihood for other family members. And the moral decay in many nations promotes the bartering and selling of children as common chattel. This crime is committed simply so children can be used to serve the desires of depraved members of society.

The adult-sized roles thrust upon children leave them with no time or energy for play, school, friends or development of relationships. Instead of a safe, healthy home and community environment, millions of children are forced to live in an environment of fear, insecurity, suffering, poverty and trauma. Their physical, mental, spiritual and emotional needs are ignored.

RESTORING GOD'S DESIGN FOR CHILDHOOD

The urgency of a compassion-driven response to the children's tragic plight is vividly described in an article written by David High following his trip to Santa Cruz. From his personal encounter with street children's sufferings experienced through murder, abandonment and exploitation, he poured out his heart:

There must be a pleading on the part of God's people all over the world that the raping and killing of these children be stopped. If our hearts do not cry out for mercy upon them, and if our hearts are not burdened by the reality of their lives, then we are a people whose hearts have grown stony and cold. It is time to bend the knee and humbly ask the Lord to take out the old stony heart and create in us a new heart of love (Ezekiel 36:26; Psalm 51:10).[2]

Yes! It is beyond comprehension to fully imagine, let alone absorb, the pain and suffering of over 100 million children living on the streets with little or no love or security from home, family or community; or the trauma of countless children who have been left homeless through war, many forced to live in overcrowded refugee camps with few necessities; or the abandonment of millions of children shunned as "dreaded" AIDS orphans because caregivers fear contracting the disease. We must, nevertheless, "ask the Lord to take out the old stony heart and create in us a new heart of love" for these children.

Our heavenly Father fully understands the pain and fear of the world's suffering children, whatever difficult circumstances engulf them. I am convinced that his deepest heart-longing is to stir us, his people, to reach out with God-given compassion toward them—the youngest members of our worldwide family. We have the responsibility to bring them the message of God's redeeming love, holistic healing and hope.

Our first response is to confront the situations children are being forced to endure by taking a "walk in their shoes." As you pursue this journey in the remaining chapters of this section, keep your hearts open to hear the children's stories. Ask God to help you feel their intense anguish from the incredible tragedies and abuses heaped on them; to gain an understanding of the hopelessness of their situations; and, above all, to sense a deep responsibility to become actively engaged in God's love and compassion toward these precious children.

Far too often in the church's ministry, children in desperate need of love and acceptance, security and hope, beauty and joy are marginal when they should be at the heart of the church's mission and identity. An Old Testament description of Jesus' ministry (and ours) beautifully portrays God's desire to have the children's painful childhoods restored to his original design:

> To comfort those who mourn, and provide for those who grieve in Zion—to bestow on them a crown of beauty instead of ashes, the oil of gladness instead of mourning, and a garment of praise instead of a spirit of despair (Isaiah 61:2-3).

May the Spirit of God prepare your heart to grasp the challenge of becoming a restorer of God's grand design for these precious little ones.

NOTES

[1] UNICEF, *The World Declaration on the Survival, Protection, and Development of Children* (1991), p. 53.

[2] David High, *Realize* (Summer: 1993), p. 2.

2

Street Children

Andy Butcher

A warm, blue-green sea laps the golden beaches, making Recife a picture-postcard destination for thousands of tourists each year. They come, take photos, deepen their tans and leave with memories of a sunshine paradise.

But away from the sand and sea front hotels, a dark shadow falls across this sprawling Brazilian city. It casts its presence over the likes of Marcia, a scantily-clad 15-year-old who stands by the side of the road, swaying under the influence of inhaled glue.

She arrived recently from somewhere in the south of the country, hitchhiking more than 1,500 miles. After an argument with her mother, Marcia decided she'd be happier on her own. She fell in with one of the growing numbers of teenagers—and younger children—living on the Recife streets. Chances are before long Marcia will sell her body to make a living in a city having one of the country's highest percentages of young prostitutes.

In Manila, Julie goes into the Philippine capital's red light district each night to find a couple of clients, the price of a meal. She usually charges three dollars but will settle for a third of that price if she has to. "I don't really like doing it," readily admits the tired 18-year-old whose "home" is a sleep-

ing spot under the stairs of a building. "But it's better to get paid for it than to have to go on doing it with my stepfather for free." Julie has been fending for herself for more than half her life.

◆   ◆   ◆

THE INTERNATIONAL CRISIS

Like many other children around the world, Marcia and Julie had dreams and hopes for the future. Now these girls are just statistics. Part of a growing international crisis, they are street children.

It's almost impossible to walk far in any of the world's big cities without seeing some sign of street children. They are found sleeping in shop doorways or begging from passers-by, many clutching an ever-present solvent container to keep them high.

Some sources quote as many as 100 million street children in the world today, facing the dangers of poor diet, inadequate shelter, crime, violence, sexual exploitation and even death at the hands of adults.

One estimate puts the number of street children in Brazil at seven million. It's said here that one in three street kids will die before his or her eighteenth birthday.

Sickness results from not enough food. Malnutrition weakens a young body's ability to fight ill-health. Accidents or fights produce injuries. AIDS becomes endemic because of unprotected sex with other street children or adult clients. And the death squads, vigilante groups who decide they don't like the dirty, possibly criminal, youngsters hanging around their neighborhoods, take the law into their own hands.

The body of nine-year-old Patricio Hilario da Silva was found in Ipanema, a fashionable suburb of Rio de Janeiro. He had a bullet in the back of his head, and a note strung round his neck which read, "I killed you because you didn't study and had no future . . . . The government must not allow the streets of the city to be invaded by kids."

Da Silva's murder, and many like it, led to a blunt newspaper advertising campaign in England by Amnesty International: "Brazil has solved the problem of how to keep kids off the street. Kill them."

While Brazil's street-kid killings are the most widely reported abuses of any country, they are in no way unique. Similar cases are documented in other South American countries and in Asia, along with countless reports of beatings, rape and torture.

Nor is the problem of street children limited to the developing world. Increasingly, homeless young people are seen on the streets of the Western world, from Hollywood to London. That trend should not be surprising, because street children are essentially a phenomenon of the modern world, a hidden export of the industrial age and the human price of social and commercial progress.

"Street children are born of the failure of development and overwhelming social pressures," observes human rights journalist Caroline Moorhead.[1] "They are there as a result of migration from the countryside into the cities, of poverty, of unemployment, of broken families and the growth of vast urban conglomerations now decaying and bursting under the weight of people."

All those pressures bear down, eventually, on the home, so what should be a haven of nurture and protection for children becomes a place of frustrated, angry adults unable to cope.

"Squatter communities, slums all around the cities, with their dirt, filth, lack of sanitation, lack of water and electricity, lack of schooling and lack of jobs—but above all, a lack of love" is Johan Lukasse's description from ten years work among street children in Belo Horizonte, Brazil's third largest city. "Most of the street kids we meet come from these kinds of neighborhoods, and the constant story we hear is one of a broken family, beatings and abuse, alcohol and violence . . . ."

20

WHO CAN NUMBER THEM?

With growing urbanization, spiraling Third World debt, rising First World unemployment and the increasing breakdown of family life—all factors that produce "runaways and throwaways"—the number of street children seems likely to grow in coming years. "Unless there is a reversal of current trends, the number of abandoned children is expected to double by the year 2000," warned the president of World Vision International, Graeme Irvine.[2]

The widely-quoted estimate of 100 million street children worldwide is tabulated by the United Nations Children's Fund and includes all youngsters living on the streets. Critics of UNICEF's figure argue that this paints an inaccurate picture. The total, they say, includes many children who may spend part of their day in the streets—perhaps working in a low-paying job—but who are still part of a family unit and return home at night. The number of hard-core street children, those who have either rebelled against or been rejected by their family and whose pillow is the concrete, is probably closer to ten million, they say.

Yet even those who encourage a more cautious estimate don't downplay the seriousness of the problem, the broken world behind each number. "Those whose only home is the street are among the most unprotected of all children," underlines Dr. Judith Ennew,[3] an advocate of more cautious statistics. "They have no power and no rights—to care, shelter, education, health."

One reason the number of street children is "impossible to calculate with any degree of confidence," concluded *Newsweek* magazine, is partly because of an attempt to hide the real picture. "In many countries the government authorities responsible . . . cling to outlandishly low estimates, apparently in an effort to deflect criticism at home and abroad."[4]

PAST AND PRESENT

Yet Western critics are warned not to be too quick to pass judgment. Italian Member of Parliament Susan Agnelli, who authored a mid-1980s report by a multinational committee established to investigate the growing street children's problem, noted "the parallel between street children of the past and the present appears in true light when one reflects that the current transformation of developing countries is a continuation of the process which began in 18th century England.

"Its evolving manifestations have reached the remote corners of countries such as Mexico and Bangladesh only now. When it is precisely such Western notions of 'progress' that have aggravated the lot of the marginal child, the West is in no position to preach about the need to cope with their consequences."[5]

COMPARING EAST AND WEST

While street children in countries like Brazil and the Philippines may be as young as seven or eight, in Europe, North America and Australia youngsters out on their own are more likely to be at least in their mid-teens.

Climate and culture both play a part in making Third World street children more evident than their First World counterparts, too. Poverty and weather make it commonplace for people to live most of their lives in the open in parts of the developing world, and working children are—if wrongly—an accepted part of the everyday scene.

Street children in the Third World raise fewer eyebrows than those in the West. Generally speaking, a youngster alone on the streets of a Western city is more noticeable to the authorities and more likely to attract inquiring attention than his or her counterpart elsewhere. Not that being more conspicuous is necessarily advantageous. Western youngsters determined not to go home, if they have one, may be forced to hide more from curious adults, exposing them to greater dangers of exploitation in the seedy underbelly of the big cities.

But for all the differences, the ten-year-old Colombian begging from shoppers and the 15-year-old German prostitute soliciting homosexual clients share "many features in common," according to Agnelli. Without ignoring the roots of economics and social effects of international debt, she concluded that "all those on the street, everywhere, can be described as victims of the crisis of the family. The breakdown of family structure and traditional values, massive emigration, the economic decline of neighborhoods in the North and the growing sophistication in the cities of the South narrow the differences between streets in different continents."[6]

THE EVER-INCREASING NUMBERS

Abandoned and homeless children were noted even in ancient times. But their numbers began to mushroom with the birth of the Industrial Revolution as countries turned from rural, agriculture-based societies to urban, industrial centers.

The appearance of ragamuffins on the streets of Europe prompted strong concern. Charles Dickens' classic *Oliver Twist* documented the dangers facing a homeless young boy on the streets of Victorian London. Victor Hugo's acclaimed *Les Miserables* did the same for Paris, noting how "disrupted households . . . disperse in darkness, no longer knowing what has become of the children, and leaving them on public highways . . . ."[7]

Periods of upheaval and social change have continued to feed the street-children population, with many "vagabond boys and girls" during the Depression earlier this century.[8] One study estimated "probably half a million juvenile hoboes moving around the highways and railroads of the United States."[9]

Clearly, "the problem is not new in human history," notes the *Encyclopedia of World Problems and Human Potential*, citing the 1800's waifs of London and New York. But "what is new is the scale . . . . The present-day numbers of street children in single cities like Calcutta may be equal to the total population of those cities in the last century."[10]

THE CHALLENGING PROBLEMS

Yet for all their growing numbers, in terms of serious study street children have been largely ignored. Only a comparative few, generally localized attempts have been made to document their backgrounds and lives. Not that the task is easy, as American researcher Lewis Aptekar found when working with a group of street children in Cali, Colombia.

He soon realized that the street-smart youngsters would readily change their story—about how they became homeless, what they did to survive, what life was like—depending on the advantage they thought a particular answer might bring. Older children will often take younger ones with them when they are begging, because they know a cute face can elicit more sympathy. Surreptitious pinches or slaps can induce the tears that encourage greater generosity from a passer-by, too.

Drugs

Completed studies reveal a disturbing picture. Sixty per cent of those questioned by researchers in Indonesia had their first contact with drugs within the first year or two of being on the streets.[11]

Work versus school

One in five street children surveyed in Paraguay work for nine hours or more a day. Many dart out into traffic at major junctions to sell newspapers, flowers or sweets. This work means they could not go to school even if they wanted to.[12]

Prostitutes

Eighty-six percent of runaways interviewed in New York admitted they had been involved in prostitution at some stage.[13]

More than one in four runaways in England said they had been physically and-or sexually abused while on the streets.[14]

THE SIDEWALK SOCIETY

For every Marcia and Julie there are perhaps ten Patricios. Boys make up a much larger proportion of the street children population. Girls are more likely to find someone willing to take them off the streets, but that shelter often comes at the high price of working in a brothel.

A glance from a passing vehicle at a group of street kids may see only a group of ragged children. Actually a clear, sidewalk-level society has its own rules and way of doing things.

The gang provides a surrogate family, where loyalty is important. Newcomers have to prove their worth, perhaps through stealing, or taking a good beating, before they are allowed into the group. Each gang fiercely protects its territory from other groups.

Street children generally view adults with suspicion. They avoid policemen and security guards at all costs, because once a street kid is known and recognized, he or she is likely to be blamed for anything that happens in the area. Anonymity spells security.

Passers-by might hand over some money or lose their purse to a snatch if they are not careful. Social and charity workers can be good for a food handout or perhaps some fresh clothes. However, the children treat them with suspicion until they have proven themselves. Sadly, harsh experience suggests that grown-ups always have ulterior motives.

That the youngsters are probably sleeping during the day does not necessarily mean they are lazy. Safety prompts them to catnap during daylight hours when streets crowded with people mean the children are less likely to be attacked or harassed. Despite being old before their time, many street children will briefly let out the child inside each of them. A hard day's work selling newspapers or a desperate snatch-

and-grab from an unsuspecting tourist may be followed by a wild game of chase in the park.

According to psychologist Anne Balfour, these actions are part of the schizophrenic nature of most street children who are "mini-adults one moment, children the next." Balfour, who spent time among street kids in Bogota, Colombia, sees beneath the bravado to the often deep-seated fear and insecurity.

And for all that they run in gangs, they are still, in many ways, on their own. "They have a real sense of 'aloneness'," says Balfour. "Not that they are lonely—there are always lots of people around them. But there is a part of them that just doesn't give to others, because they have to have some means to protect themselves from being hurt. They have to keep a little shell around them."[15]

Partly for this reason, anger is never far from the surface, ready to boil over at a perceived slight or threat. It's a sign of the hidden bruises of life on the streets beyond the visible cuts and abrasions.

"The life they live reduces their concentration so far that they find it difficult to sit still and listen," says Dr. Ennew.[16] "The frequent fights in which they are involved are a reflection not just of the violence to which they are subjected on the streets, but also of the 'short fuses' they have acquired."

Many, like Marcia, will dampen those fuses by drugs or glue. "Getting high" stills the hunger pains, whether for food or a family. But the relief is only temporary.

NOTES

[1] Caroline Moorhead, editor, *Betrayal* (NY:Doubleday, 1990).

[2] Graeme Irvine, "Abandoned Children, the Most Marginalized," *Together* (World Vision International Journal: October–December, 1991), p. 1.

[3] Judith Ennew, "Children Without Families," Save the Children Fund:1988.

[4] "Children of the Gutter," *Newsweek*, May 1, 1989, p.8.

[5] Susanna Agnelli, "Street Children: A Growing Urban Tragedy; Report for the Independent Commission on Humanitarian Issues" (Weidenfeld & Nicolson,1986).

[6] Ibid.

[7] Victor Hugo, *Les Miserables* (NY: Dodd and Mead, 1925).

[8] Joy Boyden with Pat Holden, *Children of the Cities* (Zed Books, 1991).

[9] Ibid.

[10] *Encyclopedia of World Problems and Human Potential* (Union of International Associations, 1994).

[11] Children on Jakarta's Streets (Childhope: 1991).

[12] In the Streets: Working Street Children in Asuncion (UNICEF: 1988).

[13] Joy Boyden with Pat Holden, *Children of the Cities* (Zed Books, 1991).

[14] Mike Stein, Gwyther Rees and Nick Frost, *Running the Risk: Young People on the Streets of Britain Today* (The Children's Society, 1994).

[15] Anne Balfour, a taped interview.

[16] Judith Ennew, interview by Angela Neustater, "With one foot in the gutter," *The Guardian* (December 16, 1987).

3

Sexually Exploited Children

Marjorie McDermid

In a Burmese village near the Thai border in 1992, a truck halted in front of a 14-year-old girl as she walked toward the rice paddies where her parents worked. Grabbing the child, the driver forced her into the truck. Hours later, she found herself locked up in a brothel in Bangkok, Thailand. Soon she was being raped up to ten times a day. When she cried out, a man came in and slapped her. "Shut up!" he said. "And don't try to escape or I'll beat you."

In the Sri Lankan resort of Hiddaduwa, men from London, Stuttgart and San Francisco stretch out on towels, enjoying the sun. Beside them lie Sri Lankan children. A middle-aged German strolls up to a ten-year-old boy by the shore.

"What's your name?" the German asks.

"Sunil."

The man smiles and asks, "Would you like to come with me, Sunil?"

Head lowered, the boy follows him to a cheap hotel.[1]

◆   ◆   ◆

A GLOBALLY ENDEMIC OUTRAGE

Worldwide, an estimated 10 million children are victims of today's sex industry. And the number is growing rapidly if, as reported by the U.N., one million children enter child prostitution every year.

- Of the one million prostitutes in Thailand, 80 percent are under the age of 18;
- in Brazil they number 500,000 and
- in the U.S.A. 150,000.
- Studies show that India has at least 300,000 child prostitutes.
- According to *Time* magazine, Nepal's Himalayan hill villages sell some 7,000 adolescents each year to the sweat-drenched brothels of Bombay.[2]
- In Brazil an estimated 25,000 girls have been forced into prostitution in remote Amazon mining camps.[3]
- In Manila, 15,000 children are involved in prostitution, most purchased from their parents to be sex slaves.

Child prostitution in Southeast Asia is thought of as a "cottage industry." There, girls, sometimes as young as eight years old, are abducted by brothel agents or sold by parents. In 1994 ECPAT (End Child Prostitution in Asian Tourism) reported at least one million children engaged in prostitution in Asia. A 1994 World Vision report said that 40,000 of the estimated 100,000 prostitutes in Bangkok are 14 or younger. A 1994 report from a member of TECST (Task Force to End Child Exploitation in Thailand) sets the *minimum* Thai child-prostitute count at almost 40,000. It could be as high as 90,000.

Bangkok has the dubious distinction of being the world's only completely open market for buying and selling children. The Thai government took steps to wipe out child prostitution through its child prostitution policy, proclaimed in November 1992. Nevertheless, the volume of sex trade has increased substantially in the past 10 years.

Although the sex market demands more girls than boys, the latter are not exempt. In Sri Lanka researchers believe there are at least 10,000 boy prostitutes. Each receive as little as one dollar per day.

A story from Russia told in *Time* magazine illustrates the exploitation of boys:

> Sasha, a scruffy-looking long-haired resident of Moscow, has a lucrative profession. He sells the sexual services of small boys . . . . Sasha pimps for a number of male teenagers who hang out with him near the Bolshoi, but his main "team" consists of three younger boys—Marik, 8, and Volodya and Dima, both 9.

> The three boys wound up in Sasha's clutches when they were cast into the street during the social upheaval that followed the collapse of communism. The ex-collective farmworker dresses them up in girls' clothes and sells their favors, given eagerly, he maintains, for as little as $20 a day. "I am helping them," he insists, flashing gold teeth . . . .[4]

THE ULTIMATE SEXUAL EXPLOITATION

Child advocates term prostitution the worst form of exploitation. Often called the world's oldest profession, prostitution is as ancient as the Bible. For centuries, certain cultures have used girls as temple prostitutes and practiced sexual abuse of young males for "male bonding." But child prostitution such as it is known and widely practiced today is relatively new. To some extent it is a misnomer: prostitution in adults usually finds consent from the woman, but children are entirely victimized.

The child prostitutes' problems range from threats and beatings by owners to sexual abuse by over-active customers, lack of sleep, robbery, ill health and fear of pregnancy. A girl who demands payment before going with a man is then defenseless if he begins deviant sex practices. Any child who refuses to take lower than usual rates of pay chances being taken to a "safe" place and being raped repeatedly.

WHY CHILDREN

Increasingly, adult lust for sex demands a juvenile partner. It happens in countries the world over and perhaps in places not too far removed from your home. Everywhere children serve to satisfy the lecherous appetites of sexually immature men who seek emotional release by exploiting helpless children.

Physically small and weak, children are a vulnerable, unprotected group. In Sri Lanka child prostitution was virtually unknown before the 1970s. Today, in a country where many girls are still carefully guarded until marriage, by age 6–14 numbers of them have become victims of international pedophiles.

Aside from the many pedophiles (those having a preference for sex with children), the threat of AIDS now enters the picture. Those fearing the deadly virus seek younger children—virgins—as sex partners.

Some societies believe that sex with a virgin or child can cure venereal disease. In these countries children command three times the price of older women.

TRAFFICKING IN CHILDREN

In 1987 an estimated 150,000 Nepalese prostitutes worked in India, about 20 percent of them below the age of 16. Girls are sold to brothel owners from remote, poverty-stricken areas by their parents or relatives—people whom the girls trust.

These girls, and sometimes their parents, are unaware of the sex traffic into which they are entering when they begin their long journeys, often walking for days. The girls are subjected to beatings, housed in dark rooms and poorly fed—cruelties meant to bring them into subjection to their owners. The owners expect the children to receive an average of five clients daily. Sometimes a regular client will buy a girl, "marry" her and bring her out of the brothel to deploy her in the same work and later resell her.

Foreign children in Thailand are brought in from the neighboring countries of China, Burma and Laos. As many as 5,000 per year come from China's Yunnan province. As non-Thai citizens, these youngsters have no rights. To pay for the girls' faked ID cards and protect themselves from risk of being arrested, owners force alien girls and those sold outside the country to accept more clients.

In some cases labor industries provide the market for child-sex exploitation. For example, Burmese laborers and soldiers in Thailand's Ranong province request and receive the services of Burmese girls brought in for this purpose.

Often agents deceive children into thinking they will work in a factory or home in another country. These children may be abducted, kidnapped, auctioned, sold and resold. Unlawful adoption practices also contribute to the trafficking of children to provide sexual services.

PORNOGRAPHY THE FORERUNNER

Children subjected to pornographers have their minds polluted and their innocence robbed. Their bodies are battered and their lives—not just their childhoods—are spoiled. A brochure promoting an American sex tour to Bangkok pictured the owner in a bar with a semi-naked child perched on his lap clutching her teddy bear. At an early age, these children become too old to titillate the tastes of their molesters. At this point they often feel that a life of prostitution is the only course left open to them.

Commercial pornographers profit from catering to the perverted appetites of pedophiles. These disturbed, immature people lure, abduct and blackmail children to photograph or videotape them performing lewd, deviant sex acts with adults.

Children trapped in pornography suffer unimaginable pain and degradation. Meanwhile, their sex-crazed captors indulge every erotic desire and rake in huge profits. The children are always coerced into silence about their captors' activities.

Pornographic material smuggled into Nepal is bought mostly by teenagers. In India police have raided homes, offices and hotels to find schoolgirls secretly lured and photographed while having sex with "guests." Methodically abused, tortured and blackmailed by the racketeers, the girls had been forced to solicit customers and "guests." Police reports confirmed that influential politicians were involved in the racket.

The Internet, so popular with computer users, has turned traitor on children in the realm of sex. Pornographic material is now freely available to children on the Internet. Computer bulletin boards make contact with children by learning their names and addresses and setting up meetings with them.

A Carnegie-Mellon University study reported "48.4 percent of all downloads from 'adult' commercial outlets are child porn;" and "the top two picture categories on the 'adult' market are child porn and bestiality."[5]

Pornography exploits young people in another subtle way. Photos of smiling, scantily clad, obviously wealthy starlets, beauty queens and macho male heroes lure the youths to fame in the city. Once there, the scene quickly changes, for few find their fortunes in stardom.

PROSTITUTION A PREFERENTIAL CHOICE

We may term a child's entry into the world of the prostitute as either preferential or situational. In the former, the child for some reason chooses the lifestyle. In the latter, his or her lifestyle is chosen by someone else, with no reference to the child's wishes.

Under normal circumstances few children would adopt a life of prostitution with the accompanying violence and brutalities. But under certain circumstances children choose a lifestyle that leads to prostitution.

Dysfunctional homes

Dysfunctional homes produce many runaway children who often end up living on the street by choice. Their stories vary but run along the same line: "My father is a drunkard and does not want to work regularly. My stepmother and my father have four children younger than I, and they need food and clothes. My stepmother never liked me and I decided I couldn't take that life anymore."

Personal poverty

Worldwide, the need for money lures into prostitution children from poverty-stricken homes. They may begin by being pornography models. Soon they are deeply involved in sexual practices of all sorts with their adult captors. Street children, numbering in the millions, often survive on the streets by being paid for sexual favors. (Many others are raped with no recourse or defense.)

According to a World Vision report, Belem, the port city at the mouth of the Amazon River, has the highest percentage of children engaged in prostitution in Brazil. About 23.7 percent of the girls who live on the city's streets practice prostitution. The national average is 11 percent.[6]

World Vision also reports that "city children who work to stay alive number, worldwide, between 100 million and 200 million. Sixty percent of all children in Asian cities are full-time wage earners. Child prostitution is one of the principal means of making money."[7]

The lure of the city

Urban migration accounts for another chunk of the world's youth population who practice prostitution for a living. Girls flock into the cities looking for a better life but find the labor market highly restricted. Prostitution becomes the largest economic potential open to them, especially to those who are not educated or skilled in a trade.

A 14-year-old Ethiopian child decides to make good in the big city. When she arrives, a woman at the bus depot invites her to stay at her "house." The child gladly accepts the woman's apparently kind offer. The house turns out to be attached to a bar. While the girl spends a few weeks looking for work, the woman provides her room and board. Then one day the "benefactor" buys the girl a dress and suggests that she stand on the street and wait for men as other girls do. That night the girl becomes a prostitute. She splits her miserably small "takings" with her landlady, a former prostitute. The girl still hopes to get a different job, but her lack of education or skills makes her chances unlikely.

SOLD INTO PROSTITUTION

By far the greater number of child prostitutes are sold or coerced into the sex market. The reasons vary, but the price paid by the children is just as great if not greater than those who choose this way of life.

Weak family relationships

Weak family relationships contribute to the anguish of these children. Where the home, or perhaps the country, has no concept of children's rights; where the father holds absolute power over both the mother and the children; where offspring are considered property and their salability an asset, home as we think of it ceases to exist.

Family poverty a prime pimp

Impoverished families, whether in the Americas or the East, see in their girls a way to end their indebtedness. Some may not know the horrors brought about by making chattel of their children. Many close their hearts to the pain and grasp the financial gain. Some parents, seeing how lucrative is the trade, even become flesh traders themselves.

Although prostitution is illegal in Thailand, girls sold into prostitution there bring $100–$150 (U.S.). It is reported that girls from Thailand's north send home more than $2 million per year. In the past 10–15 years as many as 70 percent of northern Thai parents who once cried for sons now hope for daughters. Parents have been known to receive advance payments for their daughters, sometimes even before the baby's birth. Trafficking in women and children is said to be more lucrative than drugs or arms dealing. Asian children are especially sought after for their "exotic allure."

Some of these girls return home when their usefulness in the prostitute "profession" peaks—sometimes as early as 16 years of age. Many of them remain prostitutes for life, earning whatever they can and feeling they have no other means of livelihood.

Religion and culture

Religious practices in some countries make prostitution appear a noble lifestyle. For example, the *devadasi* girls of India, nearly nine of ten dedicated to the gods before the age of ten, are mostly from the lower "untouchable" caste. Parents are offered large gifts of silver and promised reincarnation as high caste Brahmins for giving their daughters to the temple. "Married" to the temple goddess in a ceremony that includes animal sacrifice and religious ritual, sometimes the young child is possessed by Satan. The *devadasi* (which literally means "god's servant") is believed to *become* the goddess for the male customers paying to sleep with her. The number of *devadasis* eludes the records, but the Indian state of Karnataka alone has an estimated 100,000 *devadasis*.

Nepal's Deuki sect, rich people who desire favor from the gods, buy young girls to be offered to their gods in a way similar to the *devadasi*. Researchers claim that these girls have sexual encounters with men from five to fifteen times monthly.

Wealth and lust

If poverty is the prime pimp of child prostitution, wealth and lust is the henchman. Trafficking of children for the purposes of sexual exploitation brings incredible wealth to brothel and hotel owners and the agents who run sex tours.

To the world's penchant for satisfying every sexual desire at whatever cost, add the lust for wealth and you encounter a formidable front. The vassalizing of children to erase a family debt genders enough indignation in our souls, but the conscienceless trafficking in human flesh to line the pockets of ruthless agents must raise the ire of every true believer in human decency.

In 1994 tourism in Sri Lanka was expected to bring a revenue of up to 1 billion rupees (U.S. $20 million). A sizeable percentage of the tourists come to the island for the express purpose of having sex with children. They earn the country a reputation for being a paradise for pedophiles.[7]

Sex tours originate from many places, notably Australia, China, Europe and Japan. Many hotels and places of entertainment have a built-in sex service for foreign clients. Often it is young boys and girls who serve this flesh market.

Pedophile clubs flourish on the Internet, networking and meeting in such places as public libraries to arrange for rendezvous with children. They also provide advice to pedophiles on how to escape the law. Few pedophiles are prosecuted.

War and sexual exploitation

War also exploits children by sexual abuse. An example is the widely publicized use of rape and other forms of sexual exploitation in the Bosnian war.

Ann Noonan, assistant director of Agape Counseling Associates in Rochester, NY, says, "During times of war children are traumatized in a variety of ways through violent acts of sexual abuse. The trauma from their sexual abuse is often intensified by other humiliating experiences surrounding the event such as forced acts of incest, initiated to break down a people's strongest cultural taboos and thus the very core and fabric of their culture."[9]

CHILDREN AT PHENOMENAL RISK

The general health of every sexually exploited child is seriously endangered. Little if any health care is ever given to these children. They suffer from hunger; poor, unsanitary housing in all extremes of temperature; physical beatings and everything from the common cold to deadly infections and viruses.

Routinely, in many places, girls are put into small, dark rooms and restrained to prevent escape. Sometimes girls are sent for on request from hiding places outside brothels. Some make the headlines posthumously, such as the prostitutes who, chained to their beds, burned to death when their brothel caught on fire in a small Thai resort.

Infections

The younger the girls the more they suffer. A child, after losing her virginity on the first night, may end up in a hospital hemorrhaging, may die on the street or may be found dead on a dump. Torn up internally by adult sex partners and sometimes subjected to perverted sexual attacks, they are vulnerable to and exposed to every sort of infection. A high percentage of child prostitues are infected with some form of sexually transmitted disease (STD). Untreated, many suffer lingering illnesses and meet an early death.

AIDS

In Ethiopia a 1989 survey carried out among prostitutes in Addis Ababa revealed the prevalence rate for HIV at

24.7 percent. The most frequently infected were 15–24 year-olds. One survey of child prostitutes in Thailand reported 50 percent of them HIV positive.

"Because of the myth among older pedophiles that having sex with children reduces the risk of AIDS, younger and younger children are being lured into prostitution. Because of risky sexual practices, such as anal sex, children are at great risk of contracting the HIV virus."[10] Allegedly, HIV-positive girls repatriated to their home countries may face execution.

Social debasement

Children born of prostitute mothers, even when given a chance for education, suffer so many social taboos that they cannot cope with them. Guilt and shame force street children prostitutes into hiding. A Costa Rican street child was receiving food at a feeding station set up by the Salvation Army. Asked why his friend did not come with him he replied, "He is ashamed of last night's sexual abuse."

Children involved in prostitution rarely receive an education. School hours are not suitable, the children are too exhausted to study and usually they do not have enough money for books. They have little hope of ever pulling themselves onto a better level of living. Only someone reaching to them can give them hope.

Psychological trauma

ECPAT researchers say they have "seen no evidence that children who have been systematically prostituted for more than a short period of time can ever be successfully rehabilitated. When a child is being forced to receive several sexual partners seven nights a week, the traumatic effect appears to be impossible to overcome."[11]

Children removed from their homes and sent into alien situations suffer the most. Subjected to all the traumas of a sexually exploited lifestyle, they experience absolutely no parental love or support. Their sexual partners or their owners rarely offer anything but cursing and cruelty. If these children reach adulthood, they do so with none of their childhood traumas resolved or psychological needs met.

Does anyone care?

Although some governments are taking action, officials often look the other way. In most cases, for political expediency and to gain favor with those who bring a profitable trade to the country, governments opt to ignore the problems of children.

Currently, non-government organizations and religious organizations are being raised up to be advocates for sexually exploited children. Several of the better-known ones are featured in this book.

But the world is a big place with a burgeoning population growth producing ever-increasing, violent sinful practices. Churches and mission agencies cannot afford to close their eyes to this need. We must ask God what we can do, and be prepared to take action.

Notes

[1] Paul Ehrlich, "Asia's Shocking Secret," *Reader's Digest*, (October 1993), p. 69.

[2] Margot Hornblower, "The Sin Trade," *Time* (June 21, 1993), p. 45.

[3] Ibid., p. 45.

[4] Michael S. Serrill, "Defiling the Children," *Time*, (June 21, 1993), p. 53.

5 "Pornography on the Net," *The Church Around the World* (Wheaton: Tyndale House Publishers, Inc., October 1995), p. 2.

6 "Child Exploitation Around the World" (News brief), *Together* (April–June, 42:1994), p. 17.

7 Robert Linthicum, "Exploiting Children in Our Cities," *Together*, (April–June, 42:1994), p. 21.

8 Ibid., *Together*, p. 19.

9 Ann Noonan, "A Healing Environment for the Sexually Abused," in *Healing the Children of War*, Phyllis Kilbourn, ed. (Monrovia, CA: MARC, 1995), p. 115.

10 Ibid., *Together*, p. 19.

11 Ron O'Grady, "Ending the Prostitution of Asian Children," a paper presented at the Tenth Annual Congress on Child Abuse and Neglect, Kuala Lumpur, Malaysia, September 11, 1994.

4

Chilðren of War

Randy Miller

Every generation deserves a good war. So far, the world has been a generous provider. Bosnia, Somalia and the Persian Gulf offered the latest generation a fair sampling from the international conflict smorgasbord. The fathers and uncles of the soldiers who took advantage of these squabbles had Vietnam. Their fathers and uncles had Korea. Before that was World War II, and before that, World War I. No generation has been at a loss for a battlefield on which to test its mettle.

But lately, things seem to have gotten out of hand. In the last decade or so, the world appears to have gone overboard in its promise to stand and deliver military testing grounds to its young people. For one thing, the world has been spewing forth more wars than we can keep track of. No matter how faithfully we read our morning papers, we can hardly stay current with who is pummeling whom. Is UNITA fighting the SPLA, LRA, RENAMO or some other African acronym? How come the Afghans are still at war? Didn't the Russians leave their country years ago? Are the Serbs angry with the Chechnyans, the Croats, the Muslims or the Russians? And who are the good guys? If the Serbs are causing problems in the former Yugoslavia, then are the Muslims there the good guys? And are those Muslims different from the ones the Western media told us back in the eighties we weren't supposed to like?

In addition, everyone seems to be getting awfully pushy about wanting to jump into these tussling matches. No longer are young men politely waiting until they turn 18 to sign up for duty at their local Army recruitment offices. In Angola and Liberia, for instance, children pick up AK-47s as soon as they put down their squirt guns, although most have not made this choice voluntarily. Usually they opt for the AK-47 when the choice is to either pick up an automatic weapon or pick out a coffin.

But what seems to have been the *modus operandi* for war in our parents' and grandparents' times is no longer the case today. War is moving off the battlefields and into our cities, towns and villages. Post-traumatic stress disorder is not something a handful of war veterans suffer in silence but a condition that can be seen creeping into nearly every culture as more and more civilians are drawn into these conflicts. Once upon a time, it was the soldiers who did most of the killing and dying. Today, it is the civilians. At least they're doing most of the dying. The civilian death toll in World War I was 14 percent. This figure jumped to 67 percent in World War II. Today, 90 percent of those killed in wars are civilians and children.[1]

When war spills like ink from a bottle and seeps into the fabric of a culture, no one can escape the trauma. And it is the most tender and fragile fibers in the fabric of our society—our children—who suffer most. More children are killing and dying in wars than ever before. And the wounds they incur are neither short-lived nor just physical. They are deep and damaging, and they last a lifetime.

In Angola, nine-year-old Domingos dos Santos Luis had been living for weeks on roots, scraps of food and occasionally a piece of fruit. He was living with his 14-year-old brother, Manuel, and their older sister, Donzela, along with her year-old daughter, Marlene, in the city of Ndalatando, in the Kwanza Norte province. Much had changed, although not for the better, in the capital city since UNITA (National Union for Total Independence of Angola) had taken control of it. Domingos and his siblings were eager to leave. A friend told them that a small group of people were planning to flee Ndalatando and make their way to the government-held city of Dondo, a journey of several days through the bush by foot. Domingos and his siblings decided to go. Their party would be led by two young boys.

The journey exhausted Domingos, but the hope of a better life kept him going. On the third day of the trek, the group's young guides mysteriously disappeared. Maybe they were captured by UNITA. Maybe they abandoned the group. No one ever found out. By afternoon of the day the group's guides disappeared, the travelers had divided into two segments: those moving faster, and those slowed down by babies and children. Domingos was in the first group.

Suddenly, Domingos and his friends were surrounded by 14 UNITA soldiers, armed with rifles. The soldiers said they had been watching the group for a long time, and they believed that when they arrived in Dondo, Domingos and his friends would tell lies about UNITA to the government. This possibility had to be prevented.

The UNITA soldiers singled out the men and older boys and bound their hands behind their backs. Domingos saw that Manuel was in this group. Fourteen years was old enough for Manuel to be considered a threat in the soldiers' eyes—old enough to take up a gun and use it.

After binding the hands of the men, the UNITA soldiers took a break for lunch. When they were finished, the killing began.

The men were killed first, shot one by one. Domingos saw a soldier put a bullet in his brother, then fled for cover in some high grass nearby. After they killed the men, the soldiers bound the women and began stabbing them with bayonets. Domingos watched as his sister, whom he referred to as his *mana* (a Portuguese word indicating special affection), died at the end of a bayonet. Donzela's baby was secured to her mother's back in the traditional African manner by a broad sash of colorful cloth. A soldier clubbed the infant to death with his rifle butt.

"When I saw them kill my mana, I ran away," Domingos said. He tore through the bush until he came upon members of the group that had lagged behind. He told them to hide, but his warning was too late. UNITA soldiers noisily crashed through the bush, firing their rifles into the air. Panic sent people dashing in every direction. Domingos jumped into the high grass and hid. Several women ran past him. Soldiers ordered them to stop, threatening to shoot. One soldier grabbed a woman and jammed his bayonet into her stomach.

Domingos and a few others eluded the carnage. They hid under grass and debris for hours, listening to the screams of the soldiers' victims. Quiet finally came at sunset, and the small group cautiously emerged from their hiding place. Six adults and a handful of children were all who survived.

The small, weary band walked another three days, each night digging shallow holes and huddling under grass and branches. Six days after they had left Ndalatando, they met a band of government soldiers who welcomed them and gave them food.

Finally, in the safety of Dondo, Domingos stayed with a member of his extended family. For the first week he cried every night, keeping others awake. He had nightmares about the killing he witnessed. He was afraid that UNITA would come for him.

Today, in Luanda, the country's capital city, Domingos says he is no longer plagued by nightmares. He has plenty of good food and has made some new friends. However, according to members of his family, he still is not at ease. They doubt he will ever be able to forget the past and worry about his chances of ever recovering completely.[2]

Chances are Domingos never will recover fully. How does one get over something like seeing family members brutally murdered? It would be difficult enough for an adult, let alone a child. Today, there are thousands of children like Domingos, from Rwanda to Liberia to the former Yugoslavia. With a lov-

ing family environment and proper counseling, Domingos may be able to put his days of terror into perspective and prevent the experience from controlling his life. But it will not be easy.

Anymore, however, children are not only witnesses to unspeakable carnage, they are being forced to participate. In a report released in late 1994, Save the Children stated that some 200,000 children have been recruited to become soldiers or take an active part in war in the past decade. Children in Rwanda were forced to kill their own friends and family members in that country's orgy of slaughter in the spring of 1994. The Uganda's LRA (Lord's Resistance Army) actively recruited children, many of whom were only 11 or 12, and some were as young as five years. A January 1995 survey conducted by child psychologist Gifty Quarcoo revealed that 86 percent of the children captured and forced to serve for up to 12 months in the LRA were between the ages of 11 and 22.[3] In a December 1995 report by journalist Robby Muhumuza titled "The Gun Children of Gulu," the author states:

> Almost all the children at one time or another were ordered to torture, maim or kill other children or adults who attempted to escape or to destroy property like burning up houses. With intimidation, threats and sometimes torture, children were obeying like robots.[4]

The LRA was gender-inclusive in its recruitment, according to Muhumuza. Of the children forced into its army, 31 percent were girls, 69 percent were boys. Within days of their recruitment, the girls were assigned to male soldiers as "wives." The higher the officer's rank, the more wives he received.

Some girls escaped the LRA and received treatment at the Gulu Traumatized Children of War Rehabilitation Center in the city of Gulu. Nearly all the girls coming through the center have been infected by a sexually transmitted disease. Says Muhumuza,

When they arrive at the centre, they are usually half naked, in tatters, smelling because of not bathing, with lice and serious skin rashes. They sometimes have gun or knife wounds, swollen feet, broken bones, bruises and other infections.

They talk of recurring sad and sometimes horrifying events they witnessed, participated in or sometimes that happened to them. These include forced abduction with violence, torture and threats of intimidation, witnessing or being forced to kill with *pangas* [machetes], clubs or knives, being tortured, having to carry heavy luggage for long distances on empty stomachs with exploding land mines, or gunfire from the enemy.[5]

To its credit, the LRA was not entirely without principles. LRA leader Joseph Kony claims he received a vision from God to declare war against the heathen Ugandan National Resistance Army. Under strict instruction from the God-fearing Kony, neither adults nor children in the Lord's Resistance Army were permitted to drink alcohol, take drugs or smoke cigarettes. One must be clear-headed, after all, to usher in a government that regards the Bible's Ten Commandments as its guiding principles.

Today, there are enough big wars, internal squabbles, ethnic cleansings, tribal feuds, border disputes, soccer matches and TV talk shows to provide outlets for the violent urges in every man, woman and child on the planet. According to Save the Children, over the past decade, 10 million children—one child in every 200 throughout the world—have been traumatized by the effects of war and need help to overcome emotional distress. In its 1995 State of the World's Children, UNICEF said that in the past decade two million children have been killed in wars; up to five million have been physically disabled; 12 million have been left homeless; and more than one million have been orphaned or separated from their parents.[6]

A recent survey of 900 children in Rwanda revealed that 88 percent had experienced death in their families; 42 percent had lost both parents; 59 percent had witnessed killings and injuries with machetes; and 86 percent had found it necessary to go into hiding during the 1994 massacres.[7] More than one-third of those killed in Rwanda's 1994 massacre were children. Experts claim that up to 90 percent of the children who survived the killing remain traumatized.

In 1994, Saferworld, the independent foreign affairs think-tank and public education group based in the United Kingdom, published a book titled *The True Cost of Conflict*. In the book's foreword, The Rt. Hon. Lord Judd of Portsea writes:

> If an anthropological expedition from another galaxy arrived on earth it would surely be impossible for them to give a rational explanation of human behaviour. How would they explain why we spend 250 times more on arms than we do on peacekeeping? What would they say about the 22 million people killed in wars since 1945?. . . About the 24 million people forced to flee and become displaced people within their own countries, and the 18 million people who have become refugees abroad, all as a result of conflict?[8]

The intergalactic explorers, Judd concludes, would soon abandon such a planet, realizing there is precious little hope for it if this is how its inhabitants are treated.

The True Cost of Conflict measures our losses primarily in economic terms, and these are staggering by themselves when presented in print. The authors also present the cost in human life, discussing the number of deaths and citing examples of atrocities, much like those endured by Domingos and other civilians caught in conflicts. The authors even speculate on what might have happened had these wars not been fought. Again, in these speculations, they focus on the economic aspects. One wonders what they might say in a follow-up book that would focus on the cost in not only the number of deaths but also the damage to societies now and in the future. It may be difficult to measure; how does one quantify the effects of war on children? Different tools may be necessary—a qualitative study, perhaps—to get at some of the ways civilians, especially children, are affected by war. What is the cost to Rwanda, for example, when 90 percent of their children remain traumatized by the slaughter of 1994? It may not be possible to get a clear-cut picture, but it would be worth looking into.

Sixteen-year-old Chantelle lost nearly all her family in Rwanda's 1994 killing spree. In the chaos that spring, she and her five-year-old brother, Innocent, fled their home for a refugee camp, leaving only their grandmother behind. Eventually, they were moved to a center for unaccompanied children—actually, an old school building and a few tents. But at least they had food, shelter and health care.

In November 1995, Chantelle and Innocent returned home to be reunited with their grandmother, their only relative to survive the killings.

> [Once back at their home] Chantelle sat vacantly, taking it all in, until her grandmother spoke. Her grandmother said she had been so worried that she hadn't slept at night. She had been thinking of her children and grandchildren who had died. She listed the names of Chantelle's mother, father, aunts, uncles and brothers who had been killed. Chantelle bent her head low between her knees and wept . . . . At 15, her world had been torn apart. Today, 17 months later, it had been replaced by fragments.[9]

Domingos and Chantelle are not isolated cases "way over there somewhere." A look at what's going on in East Los Angeles, Miami, Detroit or just about anywhere in New York City will show that children are becoming armed and dangerous—not to mention frightened out of their wits—in places where it used to be safe to take an evening stroll. When children in suburban American schools have to walk through metal detectors every morning as they enter their buildings, it's time to wake up to the fact that something is wrong. Whether it's Angola, Liberia, Rwanda, Colombia, Chicago or East L.A., children are armed as never before. Most of the rest are very scared.

A review of Hillary Clinton's book, *It Takes a Village to Raise a Child*, in the *Los Angeles Times*, states:

> She argues very forcefully what ought to be self-evident: That we cannot allow the wholesale abandonment of children in unfortunate circumstances . . . . When you step back from the book, the most shocking thing is that the first lady of the United States has to argue for this at all.[10]

Certainly, war qualifies as an unfortunate circumstance. And, as the figures presented by Saferworld, UNICEF and Save the Children show, more and more children are being drawn into these "unfortunate circumstances." To sit idly by while this injustice takes place is unconscionable, especially for those who are aware of such circumstances. The plight of our children, particularly those affected by war, ought to be self-evident. Apparently it isn't. Hillary Clinton has received her share of criticism in recent years, but it is difficult to argue with her claim that we need to wake up to the needs of our world's children. If we truly care about family values, which would seem to include children everywhere, we must take a serious look at the way war is ravaging our young people's lives as never before.

After the Persian Gulf War, in an effort to help children cope with what they had experienced, Muslim religious leaders urged parents to take their children on their laps and invite them to tell all their fears and bad memories to Allah. When parents did this, they reported that their children slept better afterward.

Maybe the world should take a lesson. Our children don't need more wars, thank you very much. What they need instead is laps to hold them and ears to listen to their fears. That provision may not solve everything, but it would be a step in the right direction.

NOTES

[1] "Children Suffer in Front Line of Global Strife," excerpted from *The Guardian Weekly*, December 17, 1995.

[2] From a report by John Schenk: "Nine–year–old Witnesses Atrocities in Angola," for World Vision International, July 7, 1993.

[3] Robby Muhumuza, "Girls under Guns: The Special Situation of Girl Children Affected by Armed Conflict—A Case Study of Girls Abducted by Joseph Kony's Lord's Resistance Army (LRA) in Northern Uganda," a report for World Vision International, December 1995.

[4] Robby Muhumuza, "The Gun Children of Gulu: The Reluctant Child Soldiers in Joseph Kony's Lord's Resistance Army (LRA) in Northern Uganda," a report for World Vision International, December 1995.

[5] Robby Muhumuza, "Girls Under Guns: The Special Situation of Girl Children Affected by Armed Conflict—A Case Study of Girls Abducted by Joseph Kony's Lord's Resistance Army (LRA) in Northern Uganda," a report for World Vision International, December 1995.

6   United Nations Children's Fund, *The State of the World's Children 1995* (Oxfordshire, U.K.: Oxford University Press, 1995), p.2.

7   Tamara Martin, "Rwanda Journal: Part Two," a report for World Vision International, November 1995.

8   The Rt. Hon. Lord Judd of Portsea, *The True Cost of Conflict* (London: Earthscan Publications, Ltd., 1994), p. xv.

9   Tamara Martin, "Rwanda Journal: Part Three—My Brother's Keeper," a report for World Vision International, November, 1995.

10 Phyllis Burke, *Los Angeles Times Book Review*, January 28, 1996, p.1.

5

Child Laborers

Edward T. Bradley

Nine–year–old Rashid lives with his five younger brothers and sisters. His father has been gone from the home for three years. To help supplement his mother's income, Rashid works in a mousetrap factory six days a week, ten hours a day. The week I met Rashid, he told me he recently had a bad accident with a trap. When Rashid showed his mother the huge gash in his hand, she told him they had no money for medicine. All Rashid could do was wrap his injured hand in a cloth.

Rashid, along with other children in his slum, had put his faith in Jesus. He had been taught that Jesus would hear his prayers. The night of the accident he prayed, asking Jesus to heal his hand. At work the next day, a stranger came into the factory and walked over to Rashid's work table. The man took Rashid's injured hand, wrapped in the bloody cloth, in his own and asked, "What happened to your hand, boy?" Rashid told him about his accident. The stranger shouted for the factory supervisor who quickly ran to Rashid's table. "Take this boy to the clinic and get his hand taken care of, NOW!"

Rashid told me the man has never returned to the factory. "He must be somebody important," Rashid commented.

INTRODUCTION

I am sure Rashid's experience of a benevolent factory owner is the exception. His story, however, highlights the problems that produce child labor and the risks involved for young children. What future does Rashid have with no education and the loss of his childhood?

The definition of child labor as set forth by the International Labor Organization (ILO), in its Convention 138 on Minimum Age for Employment (1973), states: "The minimum age . . . should not be less than the age of compulsory schooling and, in any case, shall not be less than 15 years." Convention 138 allows countries whose economy and education facilities are insufficiently developed to initially specify a minimum age of 14 years. They also can reduce—from 13 years to 12 years— the minimum age for light work."[1] "Light work" is rarely defined in most countries and merely allows younger children to be employed.

Statistics on child labor are piecemeal and suspect. Many governments, especially in the developing world, lack an adequate system for obtaining accurate data on child labor. They are reticent to document activities which often are illegal under their own laws and violate international labor standards.

Child workers are found in a wide range of economic activities. The largest number works in family–based agriculture, services (domestic help, food services and street vending), prostitution or small–scale manufacturing (carpets, jewelry, garments and furniture, among others). Most children work in the informal economy that, generally, is not regulated by national law as the formal economy. This structure makes the full scope of the child labor problem very difficult to assess.

SURVEY OF CHILD LABORERS

The problem of child labor is on the rise globally. The following brief overview highlights many of the worldwide situations of child laborers.

Asia

Children in Asia work in factories and workshops where they clean and pack food, weave carpets, sew and embroider garments, glue shoes, carry molten glass, cure leather and polish gems. Children are also the invisible workers in subcontracting systems where they work in homes, small village workshops or in tiny sheds. The ILO estimates that at least half of the world's child workers are found in South and Southeast Asia.

Asian children work in tea stalls, domestic service, food preparation, grocery shops, road construction, motor workshops, hawking (everything from cigarettes to chewing gum) and as prostitutes. They also are commonly seen scavenging for and sorting garbage or crushing bricks and stones. Many street children specialize in collecting particular kinds of trash—plastic bottles, bottle caps, metal or paper board.

India has the largest child labor force in the world. Government sources estimate around 18 million or 5.5 percent of the labor force are children. Children's rights activists contest these figures and say the actual numbers are three times the government's estimate.

About 80 percent of India's child laborers work on farms or in roadside tea stalls. They work for the sole purpose of repaying parents' debts to rural loan sharks. In many rural areas young girls are sold for prostitution and brought to the cities.

Africa

The ILO estimates that in Africa 25 percent of children between the ages of 10 and 14 are involved in labor. In some countries, close to 50 percent of the children under 14 are engaged in work. The United Nations Commission on Human Rights reports that children make up 17 percent of Africa's work force.[2] Very few studies have examined the problem of child labor in Africa. Accurate data is not available.

Most children hard at work in Africa sell and trade food on the streets, wash cars, work at kiosks (small shops), serve as domestic helpers, tan and dye raw leather products, fetch water, collect firewood, herd animals or harvest crops on family farms or commercial plantations.

The next ten years will show a significant increase in the number of children in the labor force because of AIDS. In Uganda this problem has already become a concern. Many children will be orphaned and will join the ranks of street children foraging in the urban centers. Many parents will be unable to work because of the disease, and the demands of family support will fall on the shoulders of the children.

Latin America

According to ILO estimates, between 15 and 20 percent of children in Latin America work. Child labor can generally be found in home-based garment and shoe-part production, small scale mining in remote areas and, to a lesser extent, in the factories that assemble goods for export from imported materials. Many Brazilian children work alongside their parents under some of the most deplorable conditions, including forced labor and debt-bondage. In a rural area of Brazil, young children, without any protection, spray cancer-causing pesticides on tea plantations.[3] Street children in many countries are among the most abused and exploited children in the world.[4]

Another factor not included in the statistics of child labor is the need for child care because of parents, or a single parent, leaving the home during the day to support the family. Especially among the urban poor it means a child, five to ten years old, must remain at home to care for younger brothers and sisters. This child also is expected to do the basic household chores of cooking, washing clothes and cleaning the home.

COMPLEXITY OF THE PROBLEM

The ILO, in its testimony at the Department of Labor's hearing on child labor in 1994, described the complexity of child labor and issued an important challenge: "Few human rights abuses are so unanimously condemned, while being so widely practiced as child labor . . . . There is no quick fix . . . . Working children all over the world deserve better."

India's Labor Secretary S. Gopalan, speaking at a November 1995 conference on the economic implications of abolishing child labor, said industry was reticent to invest in modern technology as long as it could exploit labor at low wages. Secretary Gopalan said his country's unemployment problem could be solved if underage children were removed from the labor pool. India officially prohibited the employment of children under the age of 14 in 1948, but the law is minimally enforced.

MOST COMMON FORMS OF CHILD LABOR ABUSE

Child labor abuse is conducted under many pretenses. Debt bondage and apprenticeship afford many opportunities to provide a "legal covering of acceptance" in exploiting children for cheap labor.

Debt bondage

Debt bondage is recognized as a modern form of slavery. As Andrew Girrelli states, "Several million bonded child laborers in South Asia . . . live under conditions of virtual slavery."[5] Debt bondage is most commonly found in prostitution, domestic services, agriculture and a variety of small manufacturing industries.

The definition of slavery by the United Nations includes child exploitation involving a parent handing a child under age 18 to a business or another person for work. This handover is not only used to increase a family's income but is often a means to pay off indebtedness. Usually the child laborer works to pay off interest on a loan and never the underlying capital debt. The ongoing result is an inherited and perpetuated debt that becomes inter-generational. In India over five million bonded child laborers work to pay off family debts.

In Pakistan, debt bondage is called the *peshgi* system. Bonded child labor is common in the hand–tied carpet and the brick kiln industries. Money loans to the poor become a means of permanent enslavement because of high interest rates, manipulation of the books and low wages.[6] One story of the absolute powerlessness of those caught in debt bondage was reported by Human Rights Watch/Asia:

> Two years ago at the age of seven Anwar started weaving carpets in a village in Pakistan's province of Sindh. He was never asked whether he wanted to work. When I interviewed Anwar last November, he was knotting carpets for 12-16 hours per day, 6 to 7 days per week. He was given some food, little free time, and no medical assistance. He was told repeatedly he could not stop working until he earned enough money to pay an alleged family debt. He was never told who in his family had borrowed money nor how much he had borrowed. Any time he made an error with his work, he was fined and the debt increased. Once when his work was considered to be too slow, he was beaten with a stick. After a particularly painful beating, he tried to run away only to be apprehended by the local police who forcibly returned him to the carpet looms.[7]

In some countries, the children work alongside their parents who are under a debt contract. This arrangement is found especially on large farms in Latin America in the sugar cane fields and in the copper, diamond and gold mining industry in Africa. The London-based Anti-Slavery society states that in Thailand and Laos many children are sold outright to the highest bidders.

Because of the demand for cheap labor in the Asian cities, recruiters scan the rural areas looking to lend money to poor families. The poor families sell their children or place them under a debt security arrangement for the loan. In the Philippines, during a government raid, children as young as 11 years old were found filling cans with sliced fish at a sardine canning factory. They were working to repay the debt to their labor recruiter.[8]

Apprenticeship

One of the most controversial types of child labor is apprenticeship. The concept of on–the–job training is an excellent way to impart job skills to the young. In time, children acquire an employable skill. Actually, many apprenticeships are a form of free labor. As one commentator states:

> Learning by doing is a sound educational principle, but its economic and moral implications must not be ignored; unless procedures are carefully monitored, the free child labor force creates adult unemployment, keeps adult wages under restraint, and encourages employers to increase the work load without having to worry about the cost of overtime.[9]

Apprenticeship programs in some countries are considered educational and thus are exempt from the young age employment limits. In Egypt, for example, the underage limit is 12 years. Yet children as young as seven or eight regularly work as apprentices in carpet workshops and in the leather industry where conditions are particularly hazardous. Tasks performed by older apprentices differ little from those performed by younger children.[10] In these schemes, children work for very little pay with meals and lodging provided by the employer but deducted from their pay.

WHY CHILD LABOR?

No simple statement explains the reason behind child labor. Those who would support the use of working children cite poverty and basic survival needs as the reason for its existence. They recommend more rapid industrial growth and economic development that would remove the need for child labor.

Where technological innovation *has* reduced the employment needs for children in the organized and semi-organized segments of the economy, it has forced children to fend for themselves on the city streets. In Bogota, Colombia economic decline and mechanization have displaced both adult and child labor from the rock quarries. As a result children are undertaking petty trading and service-oriented jobs in an effort to replenish family income.[11]

Others argue that although poverty may be one very important contributing factor, other factors must be considered:

1. Economic self-Interest: Factory owners who overwork, underpay and otherwise take advantage of vulnerable child workers for the sake of profit.

2. Public indifference: Politicians, media, non-government organizations and other opinion makers who collectively treat child labor as a non-issue.

3. Public policy: Inadequate resources devoted to primary education and export promotion policies that support firms and industries without regard to their impact on child labor.

4. Government inadequacies: Labor inspectors who lack authority, expertise, numbers and accountability to enforce child labor laws.

5. Government corruption: Government officials who not only condone but in many cases personally benefit from child labor.

6. Societal prejudice: Majority groups which consider child labor among less privileged groups part of the natural order.[12]

Children work for many reasons. Some have no alternative, no educational opportunities. Others must work to survive or to meet the hardship demands of a large family.

Most apologists for child labor cite poverty as the cause. The amount of money earned by most child workers, however, is generally a small contribution to the family income. The International Labor Study states, "Although children work because they are victims of poverty, by working instead of being educated, they tend to perpetuate the cycle of poverty."[13]

SOLUTIONS

History has shown that where the more blatant forms of child labor abuse are found and closed down, children who must work to survive will find another work opportunity. Any solution for the problem of child labor must address the basic needs of the poor, the importance of justice on behalf of the oppressed, the need for children's education that will prepare them for a productive place in society and the communities' commitment to its children as an investment in its future.

The moral character of a society is reflected in the way it cares for and protects its children. Jesus' actions and teachings reflect a very high view of the worth and value of children. Until cultures reflect this same world view, the tragedy of abusive child labor will not be changed.

NOTES

[1] General Survey of the Reports Relating to Convention 138 and Recommendations No. 146 Concerning Minimum Age, Report III (Part 4B); (Geneva International Labor Organization: 1981), p. 73.

[2] "Sale of Children, Child Prostitution and Child Pornography," report submitted by Mr. Vitt Muntarbhorn, Special Rapporteur, U.N. Commission on Human Rights, UN Document E/CN.4/1994/84/, January 1994, p. 20.

[3] Brian Bird, "Children of Toil," *World Vision*, December/January 1988, p.15.

[4] Alec Fyfe, *Child Labor* (Polity Press, Oxford, 1989), p. 3.

[5] Andrew Girrelli, "Asia/Pacific Report," *World Press Review* (October 1992).

[6] *Discover the Working Child: The Situation of Child Labor in Pakistan* (Islamabad: UNICEF 1990), p. 16.

[7] *International Child Labor Hearings*, U.S. Department of Labor (Statement of Humans Rights Watch/Asia, April 21, 1994).

[8] J. Carson, *Young's Town: Prison Camp and Slave Dungeon for Child Workers* (Manila: Kamalayan Development Center, INC., Vol. 1, No. 1, July 1993), p. 1.

[9] Roger Sawyer, *Children Enslaved* (New York: Routledge Press, 1988), p. 139.

[10] Michel Bonnet, "Child Labor in Africa" *International Labor Review*, Vol. 132, No. 3 (1993), p. 386.

[11] Gary Barker and Felicia Knaul, "Exploited Entrepreneurs: Street and Working Children in Developing Countries; Working Paper Number 1" (New York: Childhope-USA, Inc., 1991), p. 13.

[12] *International Child Labor Study*, U.S. Department of Labor, 1994, p. 4.

[13] Ibid., p. 5.

6

The Girl Child

Elnora Avarientos

Shujuan, as her mother's second daughter, was an unwanted baby from birth; a baby that almost didn't survive beyond childhood. Shujuan fell victim to superstition and the Chinese bias in favor of male children. Strict population control policies limit most Chinese families to one child and, according to custom, boys are best able to carry on the family business and support aging families.

Not infrequently girls are kidnapped or sold outright into prostitution in spite of decades of public education on the equality of the sexes. Still, Shujuan's especially brutal abuse has shocked even those accustomed to hearing of the mistreatment of young girls in rural China.

To avoid fines and other penalties, her mother, Liu, did not register the baby's birth. When Shujuan was five months old, the mother gave her to another family to raise. After her mother gave birth to a third daughter, Shujuan returned to her parents' home in a village on the edge of a prosperous city.

Around the same time, a fortune teller told Liu her inability to bear sons and her husband's lack of success as a truck driver were Shujuan's fault. Subsequently, Shujuan was given only a rough cot to sleep on, deprived of food and severely beaten for "misbehavior." When Shujuan's parents took the other two daughters out to dinner, Shujuan was locked up at home. When it was discovered that Shujuan had gone onto the balcony to beg neighbors for something to eat, she was beaten for almost half an hour before someone intervened and she was taken to hospital.

"I gave birth to my daughter. She's mine to raise and mine to beat as I see fit. If she doesn't die, then I will have to die," retorted her mother.

Shujuan's abuse worsened until her mother strung the six–year–old by her hair from a ceiling fan, pulled out her fingernails and finally beat her nearly to death before Shujuan once again was rescued.

Shujuan now has no teeth, no fingernails and her eyes and lips are swollen. But she now can speak and sing songs. Her doctor reported, "We are not only treating her physical injuries, but also the trauma to her mind."[1]

◆   ◆   ◆

Girl Child. Girl Who?

This response of no recognition expresses the essence of the "girl child" born in Bangladesh, India, Pakistan, China and other parts of Asia, as well as in Africa and some countries in the Middle East. An invisible part of her society, her culture and religious heritage have reduced her to being child worker, child bride, child mother—everything but a child person. She is virtually a non–entity.

Misery and rejection

Statistics show the girl child is destined to suffer a multitude of indignities upon her physical, emotional and social person. Most likely her life will be one of misery, pain and slavery. In some poor communities, a baby girl is rejected even before she is born. If given the chance to be born alive, she is met with mourning instead of joy. Even more saddening, the

people closest to her are the very first to reject, exploit and neglect her.

They deprive her of freedom to discover herself, to have a happy childhood and life, to obtain proper health care, to receive proper education or to enjoy proper nutrition. In some communities, the daughter gets her meal only after the son gets the best part.

Her own mother may kill her while still in the womb, believing that she is a bane and economic burden to the family, not a "good investment."

Exploitation

In her early years, the girl child often will be forced to work her frail body literally to death in the sweatshops and factories of her city, or sell the same body and her soul for a pittance to support her family.

It is terrible to contemplate the waste in human resources caused by exploitation, marginalization and the death of infant girls and children because of the cultural and religious prejudice against them in their countries. Ravaged girl children some day will be mothers themselves, the nurturers and caretakers of the nation's future leaders.

The saying that "the hand that rocks the cradle, rules the world" was meant as a tribute to the female's powerful influence. What then can we expect from hands that have never known kindness and sympathy? Indeed, how many future leaders, discoverers and poets have been lost in the millions of girls turned mothers who are unable to give love because they have not known any?

Privileges denied

Education is a privilege usually denied the girl child. Although education is open to both boys and girls, boys benefit more than girls. Why? In many countries tradition dictates that education is for boys only and that girls belong in the home. Most parents believe it is useless to send a daughter to school because in the end she will only get married and look after her new family's needs. So, while still young, she is subjected to heavy household chores, working in the fields, looking after younger brothers and sisters, cooking, fetching water and performing other heavy work.

Other parents fear that education will ruin their daughters' prospect for a good marriage. It might turn them into the opposite of what a traditional wife is supposed to be, a subservient homemaker and mother.

Circumcision

The girl child usually suffers the physical maiming and emotional trauma of female genital circumcision. In most countries in Africa young girls are subjected to female circumcision to ensure their virginity until their marriage. Circumcision involves the unsanitary practice of removing girls' external genitalia by a painful operation, often with the use of unsterilized instruments, such as a sharp stone or a dull knife. The operation usually is performed without anesthesia. Many girls forced to undergo this procedure face a lifetime of complications such as painful menstruation and urinary tract infections. Even death from tetanus may result from the use of unsterilized instruments.

Eventually, the girl child will be married to a man she does not know, much less love, facing a bleak future of servitude. All in all, she will live in a world where she is in the lowest rung of priorities, with no rights and never a person to be reckoned with. Indeed, maybe her mother was right—it may have been better if she had never been born.

A CHALLENGE TO THE CHURCH

God proclaims Himself the protector, defender, advocate and redeemer of all who are broken, marginalized and down–trodden. Our Lord Jesus gave children a primary and central place in his kingdom when he stated that whoever receives *one child in his name, receives him* (Matthew 18:5). There

71

is a strong implication for the church here. It is called to participate in reclaiming those who are broken, those who continue to suffer.

The church must confront the terrible plight of these children. It must reckon with the vicious forms of child exploitation and physical, mental and psychological abuse that rob children of their dignity and humanity. The church must respond to the call to protect, defend, advocate for and heal the girl child.

These situations present tremendous implications to the church's mission and ministry priorities. It rightly has been said that the core issue is not simply one of gender or poverty. God created these children in his image, "male and female he created them." The church confronts a deep–seated societal and individual mindset that does not recognize the God–image in the girl child.

Created in God's image

A significant role for the Christian church, as leaven and salt of the earth, is to call attention to and refute strongly— yet sensitively—those cultural biases in the light of biblical truth. In the din of prevailing and entrenched cultural and social beliefs that say otherwise, the voice of the church must rise above the clamor of culture and proclaim with singular clarity the *innate value and worth* of the girl child who is created in God's image.

This injunction is neither easy to give nor obey. Any foray by the church to challenge cultural, racial or social prejudice in society is fraught with danger. A widespread perception sees the church's responsibility as mainly spiritual, the rest—social, cultural, economic, political—is the government's domain. But God calls us to care for the helpless, the defenseless and powerless where children form the greatest number. This call, then, is the mandate of the church.

Again, to battle cultural and social beliefs is to engage the church in a war against *structures and powers.* Most beliefs and practices underlying girl child discrimination are supported by traditions, rituals and laws. Studies show that many customs, taboos and superstitions which denigrate women and girls are responsible for such practices as female genital circumcision and selective abortion of girl fetuses.

Cultures which are predominantly patriarchal have, in many ways, inculcated the belief that girls are property, not persons. Politics in these cultures practically support women's non–identity and, derivatively, the worthlessness of girls.

New priorities

The church must affirm its advocacy for the girl child and translate it into visible programs of action. In its own contextual situation, the church must strive to highlight biblical truth and expose the errors of prevailing cultural beliefs and practices contrary to the expression of the divine image. It must speak out and work to change specific laws that discriminate against girl children and women. It must work to strengthen the family and promote parity in the treatment between girl and boy children. The church can work with governments to provide all children with equal opportunities for growth and development. Eventually, organizations like World Vision can work with both the church and government to achieve recognition that both women and men can be productive contributors to society.

Isaiah 65 gives a blueprint which looks to a society where there is "no infant who lives but a few days, or an old man who does not live out his years" (20a).The key is to bring "full lives" to children, girls and boys alike. In this regard, girl children need more advocacy from the church. In specific countries where girl children are oppressed and marginalized, the church should stand at the forefront with a definite bias for the girl child's welfare in the same way it has a "preferential option" for the poorest of the poor.

A justice issue

The advocacy of the church is not merely at the community level. The church should be able to engage not only its material resources but its influence and moral persuasion as well, to move governments and leaders for the needed legislation that will protect children in general and girl children in particular. Already, problems of child prostitution, child labor, AIDS, child abuse and battering exist in shameful proportions all over the world. This justice issue involves robbing and depriving the weakest member of society—the child. Moreover, injustices to girls in particular spawn more injustices to women in general. In countries where girl children are looked down on and diminished, women, too, are deprived of education, leadership opportunities and basic human rights.

We must not hesitate to take up this challenge. "Tomorrow" may be too late to heal the fatal scarring in the bodies, minds and souls of these girls. As a woman and as a mother, I cringe at the thought of what these children must endure. As a development worker, I stand heart-to-heart with those who must work to liberate parents, societies and governments from cultural and religious beliefs and structures that demean the personhood of children.

I am humbled by the thought that God used a young girl named Mary to achieve his grand design for the redemption of the world. I shudder to think how many of his grand designs may have been waylaid in the killing and maiming of these girls whom he might have chosen as vehicles for his will in the world. It is sobering to reflect on Jesus' warning that anyone who destroys or harms "the little ones" would be better off dead. Indeed, Jesus, who called little children to his side, proclaimed, ". . . the kingdom of God belongs to such as these" (Mark 10:14).

NOTES

[1] AP news report, *Child Abuse Case Shocks China*, January 16, 1996. Copyright 1996 The Associated Press. Used with permission.

7
Chilòren and HIV/AIDS

Alison Rader

Nonhlanhla Nhlapo, aged 18 months, had been abandoned by her mother at Benoni Hospital in Soweto, South Africa. She was tested and found to be HIV positive.

They brought Nonhlanhla to us at Bethesda House, a home in Johannesburg opened by the Salvation Army specifically for HIV-positive, abandoned babies and orphans infected and affected by AIDS. She was malnourished, had constant diarrhea and was eating poorly. Several times she had to be given an intravenous drip because of severe dehydration.

As director of Bethesda House, I became concerned that babies were being abandoned merely because they had been found to be HIV-positive. Wherever they were, the mothers were also severely traumatized psychologically and needed support, not rejection.

I believed that if grandparents took a step forward to look for their grandchildren, they could help the parents realize that their families do care for them. So, through the media, I made a plea to grandmothers to look for their grandchildren.

Nonhlanhla's paternal grandmother began to search for her granddaughter. Her starting point was the hospital. There she met a social worker who assisted her in her search. She finally came to Bethesda House on October 24, 1994. Overwhelmed to see her granddaughter, tears of joy rolled down her cheeks. Nonhlanhla seemed to understand what was happening. The sense of belonging was evident, because she clung to her grandmother. What a moment of reunion and joy!

The grandmother made arrangements to take the child back into the family "where she belongs." Then she began to hunt for the mother, because Nonhlanhla's condition was deteriorating: she already had AIDS. During the search for her mother, Nonhlanhla died on December 5, 1994. Her funeral was held at Bethesda with the generous assistance of Mageza Funeral Directors.

On Nonhlanhla's burial day we expected her grandmother only, but instead the families came from both sides. As these families reunited, we praised the Lord for that wonderful coming together and unconditional family acceptance.

AIDS IN SOUTH AFRICA

South Africa faces an ominous future unless all of us combine our resources and efforts in fighting the spread of HIV in our communities. Although HIV/AIDS has severe medical consequences, it is a community issue, a development issue and even a human rights issue.

According to statistics from Baragwenath Maternity Clinic, seven percent of the women attending antenatal care are HIV positive. Most of these women are aged 15–25 years and are unemployed.

Denial of the problems experienced by people with AIDS is caused by stigma, fear, rejection and persecution. These factors prevent a person living with HIV from relating to their partners, friends and families. As a result some abandon their children in hospitals.

At present Bethesda House has an enrollment of 20 babies from all over the country. Their ages vary from four months to four years. Ideally, I would like to see all these chil-

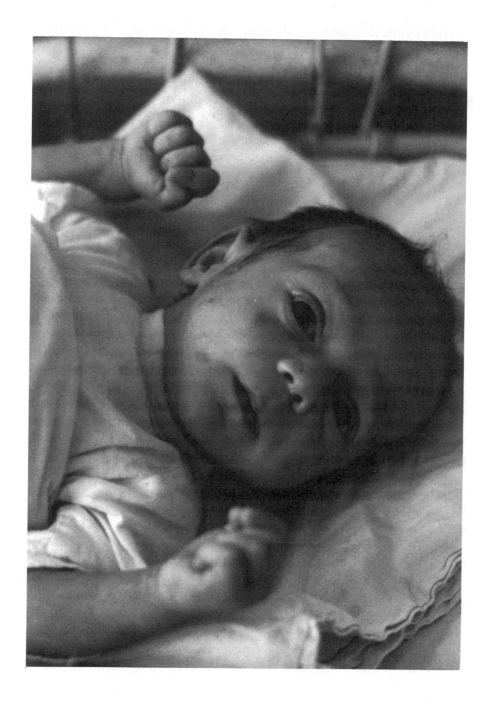

dren back in the community with families who could give them the love and care they deserve.

During the past two years we have had eight deaths in the home. For seven of them, Mageza Funeral Directors arranged the funerals for us, free of charge, helping us give these children a dignified funeral as for any other human being.

Mr. Mageza, owner of the funeral home, made this offer after hearing the sad story of the unjust, inhuman treatment one of "my" babies received. I had to go to the hospital mortuary and identify this child. For lack of funds, we arranged a pauper's funeral. I will never forget the sight as that little body was stuck into a plastic bag and the bag clipped shut with staples. I do not want anything special for these children, but I would love to see them accepted, loved and treated like all other children.[1]

GLOBAL VIEW OF AIDS

Not all babies of HIV-infected parents are HIV-infected. Several months must pass before a reliable blood testing process can happen. The mother's antibodies should have cleared the baby's system, and the test then measures the baby's own antibodies. About one-third of babies born to HIV-infected mothers acquire the infection, and of those infected about 80 percent will die by the age of five.

In 1981 AIDS was first reported in the United States of America. Today, HIV, the virus which causes AIDS, is present in virtually all countries and has infected around 18 million adults and 1.5 million children.

Sexual intercourse, whether heterosexual or homosexual, is the major route of transmission. Transmission also occurs through HIV-infected blood, blood products or transplanted organs or tissues. For example, direct blood transfusion or the use of improperly sterilized needles and syringes that have been in contact with contaminated blood may transmit the virus. Finally, HIV can be transmitted from an HIV-infected woman to her fetus or infant before, during or shortly after birth. Now in its second decade, the HIV epidemic continues to grow, invisibly, at an estimated rate of 6000 new infections each day.

The following facts further depict the spread of AIDS.

- WHO estimates that 18 million adults, and about 1.5 million children, have been infected with HIV since the beginning of the pandemic.
- By the end of the century, WHO estimates that 30 to 40 million men, women and children will have been infected with HIV.
- Today, WHO believes that 4.5 million individuals infected with HIV have developed AIDS.
- By the end of the century, developing countries will account for over 80 percent of all people with HIV infection.
- Sub-Saharan Africa, with 11 million HIV-infected, has by far the largest number of people living with HIV. But the region where HIV is spreading fastest is South and Southeast Asia, with 3 million infected adults— double the estimated number in mid-1993.[2]

Children orphaned because of HIV/AIDS

Although a home for abandoned babies is an emergency need in many HIV-infected communities, that solution is not ideal. The program in Soweto exists because the family links are not visible. One task of the program is to help uncover and strengthen family lines. The family is not only nuclear but also extended. The question is: which are the significant relationships? When a parent runs away, or dies, who are the "others"? This factor is not always immediately apparent, but must be locally explored and understood.

In Fond-du-Negres, Haiti many people have died now from AIDS. More than 3,000 orphans have been registered by the Salvation Army and the prevention work team where the catchment area has been defined as 10,000 people. At one home a man sat out in front, and his wife invited us inside the empty house. Her sister and brother-in-law had died and left their nine children with her. She already had six. Neither she nor her husband was employed. They were just waiting to see what would happen. Other households in the village were in similar circumstances.

Children with AIDS

A story from Major Jwili emphasizes the impact of caring for a child with HIV/AIDS.

Thato's mother lived in Soweto. She died shortly after Thato's birth. His elderly grandmother cared for him until she became sickly and was no longer able to look after the child.

A doctor at the Baragwanath Hospital, who is involved in HIV/AIDS treatment and a support group, took Thato to stay at her home for a period of two months. He was very sick and needed much attention. Although Thato improved considerably, the doctor could not continue looking after him. She contacted us and the boy was placed at Bethesda, where the grandmother often visited him.

On admission Thato was relatively well. From a developmental view he had delayed milestones. His condition improved. He started eating, though slowly and reluctantly. He also began walking about, exploring the vicinity and communicating with other children and staff.

Two months after his admission, his grandmother came to visit him, accompanied by her younger daughter, Thato's aunt. The child was cheerful and active during their visit.

We discussed with them the importance moral support and family life hold for all of us. Thato needed that support, too. His aunt then requested that she be allowed to take Thato to stay with her on weekends. We arranged visits and she eventually took Thato to stay with her.[3]

80

SAFETY AND DEVELOPMENT FOR CHILDREN

HIV/AIDS will "set back the clock" on primary health care successes of the past fifteen years. Infant mortality will increase. Birth rates are increasing, in part as a result of increasing mortality. Average age of death and life expectancy will decrease. Women are increasingly affected, which means children will be also.

Children have various sources of risk for their own infection. Sources can be parental transmisson or breast feeding if the mothers are infected; sexual abuse; sexual experimentation, as they reach puberty; and intravenous drug use. Children who are not *infected* may be directly *affected* by the death of parents or other family members or by the inclusion in their family of other children whose parents have died.

The awareness of HIV may have a preventive influence, or children may feel helpless to avoid infection themselves. Whether infected or affected, children need safe places and relationships to help them understand what is happening.

RESPONSE TO THE PROBLEM

As indicated by the previous chapters, in addition to this one, children are facing many problems. How do these different problems all point to the same roots of poverty, abuse and changes in community values?

Community change

Community life and norms have been affected in such a way that children are not protected in the way they should be. In response to different issues, and in particular to HIV/AIDS, it will not be sufficient for the church to conduct programs geared only to children. It will not be sufficient for social services to be established. This fact is particularly clear in developing countries where the strongest infrastructure is family and community. Yet, it is also true in countries of the West where community is more difficult to define and identify.

Collective responsibility must be rediscovered and reasserted. How can Christian responses be an enlivening influence within communities so that the outcomes include an increase in shared responses and stabilized or reoriented structures?

Christian response can have a helpful effect in the lives of these children. As communities accept collective responsiblity, fundamental changes in the attitudes, behavior and environment surrounding children begin to emerge.

Welfare or restoration?

Are economically and socially depressed communities only to be pitied? How do organizations work in such contexts so that the decisions rest with the community members and not with outsiders? This distinction marks the line between relief and development work. Relief may function independent of the choice-making capacity of people, because they are in crisis or severe constraint, and immediate needs must be met.

When a community is in crisis and the subject is children, the responsibility and right to choose remains with the community. It is possible for people in programs to see the community as too weak or helpless, because of a lack of resources, to implement decisions. A strong mutual respect is needed between programs or organizations and communities to work together for solutions and bring outside resources into the process of community choice-making.

A community in Haiti has been discussing action they could take to provide more support to the children whose parents are gone. One of the churches is "hosting" by providing land for a canteen being built by community hands. One meal per day will be provided there on a cooperative basis, for the children in most need. This is not a wealthy village. Just down the hill from the canteen site is the only water source for the village, which is a tiny spring, barely trickling a few inches. Many people crowd around, waiting for their turn to coax water into bowls.

In some communities many families are headed by children. The grandparents and adults who remain have organized to pass on knowledge and skills to the children. Farming and marketing skills as well as family-life norms are being shared by people who did not previously have the role.

Economic survival is one dimension. If they are not adults when their parents die, children may not have the right to their inheritance of house or land. Health and education needs are a particular concern when parents are not present to provide them or be advocates. Children who are surviving without parents have many challenges, including the burdens of sorrow, grief, fear of the future or—more frequently—hopelessness about the future.

JOURNEY INTO HOPE

In practical terms, bringing hope to AIDS children and orphans means the social worker is now reaching for a different vision. He or she, along with team members, is talking with members of the community and looking for a way to meet together as a whole to discuss the children's future. Community members as well as the workers can be affirmed in their responsibility as decision-makers rather than only burdened by the physical responsibilities of care without resources. The Salvation Army will then be better able to discern its role in supporting community-determined strategies for care and protection of the children.

The process that the team in Haiti is pursuing, like many teams around the world, is called "community counseling." This profoundly Christian interaction uses counseling skills and approaches to help whole communities begin to accept the realities of HIV. The counsel does not just offer information nor assume the responsibility belongs to certain organizations but emphasizes personal and corporate responsibility.

What are these realities? That HIV/AIDS is now a permanent part of the future and that all of us are being changed by the experience. Change of a positive kind is the work of the

Holy Spirit—on counselors or on communities. We participate in that spiritual reality. Bearing stress is replaced by sharing the struggle and the growth. Joint exploration and articulation of truth bring liberty and light to the process so that healthy choices for change may be made.

NOTES

[1] Nonhlanhla's story and information on Soweto provided by Major Linah Jwili, director of Bethesda House, The Salvation Army, Johannesburg, South Africa.

[2] Sue Armstrong and John Williamson, "Action for Children Affected by AIDS, Programme Profiles and Lessons Learned," WHO/UNICEF, Joint Document (1994).

ADDITIONAL RESOURCE MATERIAL

Campbell, I.D. and Rader, A. "HIV Counselling in Developing Countries: The Link from Individual to Community Counselling for Support and Change," *British Journal of Guidance and Counselling,* (Vol. 23 (1) 1995).

Chevallier, Eric with Flour, Gagnard and Roxby."Support to Children and Families Affected by HIV/AIDS," Report of Lusaka Workshop organized by International de l'Enfance with support of French Ministry of Foreign Affairs. Available from UNICEF, New York.

Reid Elizabeth. "A strategic approach to assisting children whose parents know they are HIV-infected, are ill, or who have died of AIDS," presented at 8th Workshop on Management of Field Co-ordination for Senior UN System Representatives from LDCs (1993). Available at United Nations HIV Development Program, New York.

Part 2

A Biblical Response

8

It's Time for Children Everywhere

Jennie Woods and Sandra Levinson

"Don't you see that children are Yahweh's best gift?
The fruit of the womb his generous legacy?
Like a warrior's fistful of arrows
are the children of a vigorous youth.
Oh, how blessed are you parents,
with your quivers full of children!
Your enemies don't stand a chance against you;
You'll sweep them right off your doorstep."
Psalm 127 The Message (paraphrased Scripture)

Of all the gifts God gives us, he tells us that *children* are the very best! All children are his very best. Every child was created in the image of God the Father. *Every* child has a hope and a future in Christ and in God's eternal family. When Jesus walked on the earth, he had some pretty radical statements to make about children. "Unless you are converted and become as little children, you will by no means enter the kingdom of Heaven."[1] Jesus was basically saying, unless you become like one of the children . . . forget it! You can't enter in. Our Lord loved children!

Just imagine Jesus with children all around him. Do you think he bent down to touch their faces? How about sitting on the ground? Did they climb up on his lap, put their arms around his neck or pull his beard and hair? Did they interrupt him while he was teaching, and try to run and sit on his lap? Were they quiet, as they are supposed to be in church, or loud and rambunctious?

One day, when Jesus had finished answering the Pharisee's questions, doting mothers brought their little ones to him, asking him to put his hands on them and pray for them. What nerve these mothers must have had! They walked right past the great teachers of the law, boldly interrupted the scene and coaxed their clinging children to reach out to Jesus. The Pharisees were shocked. So were the disciples! Wasn't it obvious the children were distracting the Master and wasting his time? The disciples shooed the children away and rebuked the ambitious mothers. Surely they could manage to take care of their own children.

But Jesus called the children back. "Let them come to me," he said, "for of such is the kingdom of heaven."[2] The Lord of Glory stopped his "important" work to bless the children.

What was Jesus talking about when he said that the kingdom of heaven is made up of those who are like children? Imagine, Jesus using *children* as examples for adults! Was he referring to their simple faith and complete trust that for them is as natural as breathing? Or was he asking us to imitate their humility and fresh point of view? Children are not shy about asking questions, and don't they always have plenty of time to devote to the things they like to do? Best of all, they love to sing, laugh and play. Perhaps Jesus was saying that these delightful, childlike qualities should be imitated.

Jesus not only blessed children, he also *honored* them. In royal processions the most renowned dignitaries, the cream of the nation, are given the awesome distinction of preceding the king. It wasn't just by chance that children led the Lord of heaven and earth into Jerusalem for the last time before he was crucified. Children were expressly chosen for this distinction. Will children be the ones to usher Jesus in at his second coming? We know they can offer perfect praise[3] and can defeat the enemy with their prayers.[4]

Children, so honored by God, are often held in low esteem by adults, as evidenced by the following statement that appeared in the *Chicago Tribune*: "My husband and I are either going to buy a dog or have a child. We can't decide whether to ruin our carpets, or our lives."[5] While DINKs (Double Income, No Kids) may be in vogue in the suburbs, the fullness of the earth still belongs to the Lord Almighty.

No *accidents* are conceived. No *mistakes* are born. When a child is ignored, damaged or left to die, all the world and each of us suffer the great loss of what God intended that child to be. In the face of glaring ingratitude, and even hostility, God continues to give his very best gift to a world that does not understand or value it.

Consider the statistics: when we delve into the reality of life for children, we discover that they make up the largest and most disadvantaged segment of all humanity. One in three people alive is under the age of 15. It is estimated that over 80 percent of the world's young people—1.4 billion—are growing up in non-Christian settings.[6]

Today, children are a "silent" emergency. They are silent because they are hidden within the bowels of society, with no means to raise their voices and speak out in their own behalf. They have no organizations lobbying for them, nor do they have the ability to organize themselves to protest their lot in life. If someone doesn't speak out and act on their behalf, their difficulties will escalate and their destinies disappear.

If the children of the world *could* speak for themselves, what would they be saying?

- 200 million of us who are under the age of five suffer from chronic hunger. Every day 35,000 of us die because we do not have enough to eat.[7]

- More than 25 million of us don't have even a hovel to call home. We live on the streets.[8]

- Millions of us are working up to 16 hours every day of the week in deplorable conditions and paid almost nothing.[9]

- In the United States alone, more than three of us die each day as a result of child abuse.[10]

- My parents had to sell me because they couldn't afford to feed me.

- My parents forced me to beg on the streets to buy them drugs.

The list of horrifying atrocities against children would fill a book. In the past 10 years, 1.5 million children were killed in wars. Four million were blinded, brain damaged or permanently maimed.[11] In Brazil, children are shot on the streets because they are pests. In Africa orphaned children roam the streets, bellies swollen, eyes vacant, hope gone. Why?

In several warring countries, boys as young as six are kidnapped into the army and forced to commit horrible crimes. In nation after nation, including the United States, children are as disposable as diapers and annoying as buzzing flies. Why?

Perhaps this generation of children is being oppressed as no other has ever been *because they are chosen*. Could it be that as we approach what many consider to be the end of time, *this* youngest generation is *the* generation chosen to announce the second coming of the Lord?

Since ministry to children was never more important than it is right now, *why* is so little attention given to evangelizing and rescuing the world's children?

The opposing question is *why* "waste" the enormous amount of time, energy and expense on children who aren't old enough to really understand anyway? Is it not wiser to wait until they get past their childhood foolishness and can really be taught the Word of God? Is it not more strategic to teach the parents and let the parents teach the children? It is no wonder that strategy planners in missions traditionally turn their energies to adults.

And what about individuals—you and me? "Children tie the mother's feet," said Amy Carmichael, who rescued temple children in India from 1901 until her death in 1951. Amy struggled with her own leading to *settle down* from evangelistic touring to take on the role of "nursemaid." She wrote, "The new work seemed poorer than the old . . . . Could it be right to turn from so much that might be of profit (evangelistic tours, convention meetings for Christians and so on) and become nursemaids?" The work with children would require great self-discipline and effort. However, she goes on to say, "We let our feet be tied for love of him whose feet were pierced."[12]

What would happen if each and every one of us "tied our feet" because we value and love children enough to bring them the gospel, healing and discipleship? What would happen if we invested our collective energies, talents and resources to care for the hungry, lonely and outcast children in this world? What would be the impact? Who can guess? *No* force can stand against the power of God's love! One thing is sure: there would be no more "business as usual."

For a moment just imagine you are going out somewhere in the world to pick up a starving street child. When you return you bring him or her into a gathering of adults. It doesn't matter if that adult group is comprised of businessmen at a board meeting, teens at a party or seniors at the Elks Club; whoever these people may be, they will likely stop what they are doing and all interest will focus on your child. Several will offer to give your child a bath while others will leave to bring back a delicious, nourishing meal. Medical care will not be hard to locate, and you will have more than one offer of clean clothes and a warm, clean bed. Within a couple of days, your child will have dozens of wonderful, qualified families competing for the privilege of adopting him or her. A life will be changed because you went out of your way to make a world of difference in the life of one child. The problem is we can't go out and pick up starving children and deposit them in front of potential benefactors. It's a huge job! Where in the world do we begin?

Remember the battle to save the whales? Not long ago, almost all the whales were gone. Hunted and slaughtered until only a small number of them remained, they were an "endangered" species. If something wasn't done, and done fast, there would be no more whales. The world at large did not know, *or care*, that within a few years there would be no more whales.

It was a big problem. If the whales were going to be saved, all the countries of the world would have to agree to stop killing them. The fishermen who made their living hunting whales would have to find new sources of income, and the whale products industry would have to either find new products or close their doors. Lots of people said, "The problem is too big . . . nothing can be done." But think back. It seems like everyone heard about the slaughter of the whales and everyone everywhere across the earth was asked to take part in a whale survival program. And many did! A powerful grassroots movement swept across this nation and around the world. People wrote letters, raised money, signed petitions, prepared interviews, produced documentaries and sold T-shirts and bumper stickers.

Because people cared enough to speak out loudly on their behalf and do something about their plight, whales once again filled the oceans, and they have been removed from the endangered species list.

What about the "endangered children" the world is losing? They are within our grasp. Are they worth the energy and expense invested to save the whales? Let us all stop asking *why*, and start asking *how*! There can be a great harvest of children, those so near to the heart of God and to his kingdom.

It's time for Christians everywhere to start a grassroots movement on behalf of the world's endangered children. Everyone must get in on it! Each one of us, with one strong, loud voice must proclaim—

IT'S TIME FOR CHILDREN EVERYWHERE!

NOTES

[1] Matthew 18:3 NKJ.

[2] Matthew 19:14 NKJ.

[3] Matthew 21:16 NKJ.

[4] Psalm 8:2 NKJ.

[5] Rita Rudner, *Chicago Tribune.* Quoted by Mark DeVries, *Family-based Youth Ministry* (Intervarsity Press, 1994), p. 88.

[6] World Population Data Sheet, Population Reference Bureau, 1992. Quoted in *The Changing Shape of World Mission*, Bryant L. Myers (MARC 1993), p. 40.

[7] James Grant, *Food, Health and Care* (UNICEF, 1994), p. 1.

[8] James Grant, *State of the World's Children* (UNICEF, 1991). Quoted in *The Changing Shape of World Mission*, Bryant L. Myers (MARC 1993), p. 32.

[9] *Stolen Childhood*, a special report by Cox Newspapers, June 21–26, 1987, back cover.

[10] David Wiese and Deborah Dars, "Current Trends in Reporting Fatalities: The Results of the 1994 Annual 50 State Survey," (National Committee to Prevent Child Abuse: 1995), p. 14.

[11] Barbara Thompson, "Children of War," *World Vision* (April/May 1995), p. 4.

[12] Amy Carmichael, *Gold Cord* (Christian Literature Crusade, reprint of 1932 edition), pp. 40–41.

9

Church Planting Among Children: Biblical Directives

Timothy Monsma

In biblical times children often carried out important assignments. Miriam helped rescue her brother Moses (Exodus 2:4–9). The boy Samuel conveyed God's revelation to Eli (1 Samuel 3). Joash became king of Judah at seven years of age (2 Kings 11:21). And a young slave girl from Israel helped rescue Naaman, the commander of the Syrian army, from leprosy (2 Kings 5:2-3).

In New Testament times Jesus provided food for thousands when a boy had the forethought to take with him bread and fish (John 6:9). The girl Rhoda announced Peter's miraculous presence at a prayer meeting (Acts 12:13-14). And Paul's young nephew worked to save him from harm when he was captured in Jerusalem (Acts 23:16–19).

Because of God's view that children are important, one is not surprised to hear Isaiah say, "He gathers the lambs in his arms and carries them close to his heart" (Isaiah 40:11). Jesus rebuked his disciples when they started to send mothers and their children away (Mark 10:14). "And he took the children in his arms, put his hands on them and blessed them" (Mark 10:16). Jesus also used a child as an example of humility before his disciples (Matthew 18:1–5).

The pro-life movement is built on the premise that children are complete members of the human race even before they are born. If they are complete human beings created in God's image even before they are born, and I believe they are (Psalm 139:13–16), how much more are they human beings with worth and dignity in God's eyes after they are born.

Some evangelical Christians argue that the relationship between Old Testament circumcision and New Testament baptism is so close that babies ought to be baptized. Other evangelical Christians argue that baptism is built on a personal and conscious profession of faith in Christ. Therefore, they conclude, baptism ought to be withheld until a child is twelve or older and can be trusted to make a personal and credible choice.

Both groups agree on the importance of children in God's eyes. Those who wait with baptism have a service of dedication shortly after a child has been born. They also begin to instruct children in Sunday school and in other ways even before they are school age. If children of believers are important in God's eyes, other children are by implication also important, for it is God's will that the good news of the gospel be told to all creatures.

In citing the importance of children, I'm assuming that all children from birth through seventeen years of age are included. From this perspective we will reflect on children in the church, the school and the Christian community.

CHILDREN IN CHURCH

When numerous first-born children were killed in the last plague on the Egyptians, the Israelites were celebrating the Passover with their children and explaining it to them (Exodus 12:26-27). Children were involved in the sacred assemblies called by God in the wilderness and certain ceremonies and monuments were partly teaching devices for their benefit (Exodus 12:26-27, Deuteronomy 11:19-20, Joshua 4:5–7).

It is not surprising, therefore, that when synagogues arose among the Jews, they were used during the week as schools for Jewish boys. Assuming that the normal pattern of instruction was followed, Jesus and the disciples learned to read and write in the synagogue schools. While still young they participated in worship services on the Jewish Sabbath. When Christian worship began, the pattern of including children continued. Young Rhoda went to open the door when Peter was knocking because she too was at the prayer meeting (Acts 12:12-13).

It can be concluded that Christian worship would have been incomplete without at least the older children present. The presence of children forces the speaker, if sensitive to the audience, to explain Bible passages in simple words and concepts. This response to the children assures that all adults catch the meaning as well, including those who might be ashamed to complain, "You are talking over our heads."

Many married couples without children earnestly desire them. Children are a normal part of family life in the home. The family of God also includes children.

The implication for church planting efforts is that we should aim for churches that embrace all ages. Churches that deviate from this pattern are incomplete. We ought to ask, therefore, how we—even in our initial evangelistic efforts—can make provision for children.

CHILDREN IN SCHOOL

Many traditional missions have made extensive use of schools to reach entire communities for Christ. Beginning with primary schools, they have in time expanded to include secondary schools and even college level education.

Donald McGavran and others have criticized these schools as institutions that demand heavy investment of money and personnel but don't yield fruit in proportion to the investment. I'm sure this was often the case in India where McGavran worked. Educational efforts among native American children have encountered similar problems. But in much of Africa the story has been quite different. Most Africans are more enthusiastic about formal education than many Afro-Americans. Many African children first heard and responded to the gospel in a school setting. Some African missions that didn't sponsor schools were able to plant churches rapidly only because they were proselytizing the graduates of other mission schools.

Nowadays the discussion over the value of schooling as an evangelistic and discipleship tool is fading because most schools, even those that began as mission schools, are now government controlled and financed.

But the point is this: traditional missions have been involved with children for a long time through the educational systems they have fostered. If such missions would now shoulder the task of ministry to the more than 100 million children who are at risk in this world, these mission programs would be no novelty from the point of view of ministry to children. They would be a novelty only from the point of view of *the type* of children who would now receive their attention.

Missions have been willing to work with children in the past because they knew these children represented the future leaders of church and nation. They also knew that the transition from child to adult occurs quickly. Children 10 years of age today will be voting, working, fighting (in armies) and child–bearing adults within 10 years time, if not before.

Some cases, such as Rwanda, need extensive orphanage work. Even then the number of orphans tend to overwhelm the system because of all the fighting and killing of adults that has taken place there. A great need for orphanages and foster homes exists in Mexico and Brazil as well. Some street children sleep with a single parent in a shack somewhere. Others simply sleep on the street. In either case their most pressing need is not for lodging, but for attention from missionaries and other Christians during daylight hours. While drop–in centers, feeding programs, medical help and camps for children are all helpful, these children need training in reading, arithmetic and Bible knowledge if they are ever to become productive and responsible members of society. Orphanages also provide schooling for their children, either inside or outside the orphanage. The training they receive resembles the training children once received in mission schools.

In 1993 I was at a camp for street children sponsored by Action International Ministries and Christian Growth Ministries in the Manila area of the Philippines. The program of the camp actually involved a great deal of informal training for the children, although it was given in a camp setting rather than a school setting. Children learned promptness and discipline in arriving at the various events on time and in cleaning up after themselves. They were taught songs, Bible stories, Christian ethics, public speaking and acting. They were also trained in the give and take of small group discussion and in sports. Thus, at camp the street children learned several functions often taught by schools. It became a sort of an informal school for the children. It approached the type of work in which many traditional missions have been involved for a long time.

From the first century onward, churches have traditionally included children in the worship services. When the inclusion of children in worship is supplemented by sound education, genuine and rapid church growth is likely to occur. Therefore, attention to children is not a bothersome excursion down a deadend road; it's part of the superhighway over which contemporary missions ought to be traveling.

CHILDREN IN THE CHRISTIAN COMMUNITY

Street children by definition live in a city. Most orphanage care is given in or near a city. The question of the integration of children who desire to follow Christ into the Christian community is a question to be answered with this urban environment in mind.

But when we have said "urban environment" or "metropolitan environment" (here treated as one and the same), we have already suggested a way in which the integration can proceed. Children are not the only people in cities who may be at loose ends; many adults are also "down and out." Unless one has good networks, the city can be for all a very lonely and dangerous place.

The goal of the integration of children with adults is an institutional church and a Christian community that embraces human beings of all ages. It is not a church just for children, for such a church would be very incomplete.

Missionaries and evangelists sometimes specialize in ministry to specific adult groups such as prostitutes, drug addicts, soldiers, prisoners and others. When prostitutes turn to the Lord, the goal is not a church made up exclusively of former prostitutes. The goal is rather the reintegration of former prostitutes into mainstream society. Many who were forced into prostitution by trickery or intense economic pressure earnestly desire to marry and live normal lives. Even those converted prostitutes who never marry desire to support themselves by way of legitimate work.

Not all children can be integrated into existing families. With some younger children, joining a family is a viable option. But the older these children are the more difficult it generally becomes to place them successfully in private homes. Even putting them with their blood relatives may spawn problems.

Assuming that some children will continue to live in a group setting, and some may continue to live on the street or under a bridge, the Christian community is nonetheless a place where children can receive some of the tender care that other children receive at home.

The existence of homeless children in the midst of a Christian community is a test that allows all Christians to prove the sincerity of their faith. "Do not forget to entertain strangers, for by so doing some people have entertained angels without knowing it" (Hebrews 13:2). "I tell you the truth, whatever you did not do for one of the least of these, you did not do for me" (Matthew 25:45).

100

The reception of needy children by the Christian community has two phases. The first is a witnessing phase to those children who are still strangers to the faith. Children who were mistreated by foster fathers or who ran away from their own drunken fathers, may have trouble grasping the biblical teaching of the Fatherhood of God.

A new, patient, Christian "foster" father may have to demonstrate what true fatherhood is all about. He's not a foster father in the sense that he adopts these children or even invites them to live with him. But he and his wife invite them into their home, they visit the children in their "home" wherever that may be, or they meet with them frequently at a neutral location.

The second phase of integrating children into the Christian community is the enfolding phase. Here those who have made a Christian profession are embraced as young brothers or sisters in Christ and shown the love that Christ commands. This process might be the more difficult because the young convert might still have rebellious ways even though he or she now has a new heart. Disappointments are almost bound to occur. Tough love and patience must be combined as the process of Christian nurture goes forward.

Sometimes the adults who seek to help needy children are themselves "children in Christ" because they are new to the faith. We encountered that situation in a city in Mozambique where my wife and I worked with five other volunteers for one month. The Mozambican supervisor, however, did not give up. She patiently worked both with the adults and with the children, encouraging all to grow in Christ and serve him. I supplemented her efforts by teaching these volunteers the biblical concepts of sin, salvation and service.

When new Christians volunteer or are asked to work with difficult children for the sake of Christ, it can become for them a proving of their faith. Their faith can grow as day by day or week by week they prayerfully face the challenges at hand.

CONCLUSION

Those who embark on this adventure for God may initially encounter difficulties. Unforeseen problems may arise and middle class Christian adults may be reluctant to associate with what they consider the scum of society.

But in the past Christians have undertaken, and even now are undertaking, difficult tasks. Think of the difficulty of witnessing for Christ and building churches in the communist nations of Asia. Think also of the hardship and risk of planting churches in Muslim lands. Some of us try, anyway, out of obedience to Christ.

The children at risk in our world—more than 200 million of them[1]—are a gigantic social group virtually unreached with the gospel. They will be among the peoples (LAOS in Greek) mentioned in Revelation 7:9 standing before God's throne with white robes, because some Christian missions of our generation have shown others the way.

NOTES

[1] The most recent UNICEF reports indicate more than 200 million children at risk worldwide.

10

Integrating Children's Ministry into Mission Philosophy

Howard Brant

The United Nations has pointed out that the children of the 90s will b· the largest generation ever entrusted to humankind. In aı even greater measure, I believe God has entrusted them to th care of the church. The plight of the world's children and urgent need for churches and missions to respond mo. iblically have already been highlighted. I would like to shar w SIM International, a traditional church-planting mission, was led to rethink their strategies and mission policies, making ministry to children in crisis more central to their task.

In late 1991 Dr. Kaleb Jensen, working with the Adopt-a-People Clearing House, came to speak at an SIM senior management team meeting. Kaleb laid before us the population growth figures of the world. He described what the world would look like by the year 2020 A.D., pointing out that the figures represented the greatest unreached people group that has ever come to Planet Earth. Kaleb encouraged us to think strategically about these people.

We probed Dr. Jensen's thinking concerning what SIM should be doing about reaching this massive new population coming into the world. Kaleb gave a response that really shocked us: "You have to reach the women and the children."

Dr. Jensen's response came on the heels of a similar challenge being voiced by Doug Nichols, international director of Action International Ministries. He was pleading for missions to respond to the overwhelming needs of the 100 million street children worldwide. Keith Myers was also writing concerning the children's tragic plight on a global scale. Dr. Jensen's challenge, and other leaders' growing concern over children in need, set in motion several things in the mission. SIM had gotten the message.

For us it was a philosophical shift because, until that time, we were not viewing children and womens ministries as a priority. I think our current missiological thinking had been based on the church growth models that suggested we had to reach the opinion makers—the "important" people. We were thinking that ministries to women or children were not very important.

Coupled with that idea was the fact that the fastest growing populations in the world are Muslim. We felt that to simply concentrate on women and children in the Muslim context did not seem the best strategy for reaching them. We were concentrating on the males, particularly family heads who have the say in their homes.

In some areas of the world, we felt we should *not* work among women and children. If they became the primary group of believers then most of the men and families would reject Christianity as "simply women and children's religion."

In 1992, in our International Council, we presented the findings of Kaleb Jensen and came to the conclusion that we must change the focus of SIM. Instead of a non-emphasis on childrens and women ministries, we would lift women and childrens outreach to a priority position of emphasis within our agency. We did this by a motion in our council that stated:

It was moved, seconded and approved unanimously that:

a. SIM make a proactive position toward reaching the masses of children being born throughout the world.

b. each SIM field propose a strategy for reaching the present and the upcoming new generation of children.

c. every SIM area review its strategy on women's work and consider the appropriateness of involving single and married women in such ministries.

d. SIM encourages and enables our emerging churches to meet the challenge of the new generation.

e. we specifically encourage our related churches to open and operate church schools that can be administered by the churches and financed through local fees.

That was the official council minute formulated in 1992. Along with that minute came a statement in our Consolidated Strategy Statement of 1992. One plank of our 11-point strategy was titled, "Focusing on Ministries to Women and Children." It stated:

Being aware of the anticipated 4.5 billion children who will be born in the next thirty years, we recognize a strategic opportunity and responsibility. Women and children represent one of the most neglected but open segments of society. Women are the key to the home and to the next generation. We will seek ways of addressing this challenge, including the ever-growing number of homeless women and street children.

This policy went into effect throughout SIM. We did not try, however, to dictate throughout the organization how this would take place; instead we watched as each of our field councils began to take this policy seriously.

Before 1992 we had few, if any, requests for new personnel to work specifically in children's ministry. Suddenly on our "needs lists" from around the world we saw requests for people to work with women and children. As these requests were made known, we found that volunteers were quick to respond.

Very soon we had a lady, who had been working with the Salvation Army in New Zealand, offer herself to go to Sudan to begin work with the street children of Khartoum. Others began to pick up this concern in different cities like Addis Ababa in Ethiopia. Both mission and church groups started thinking about what we could do together in partnership for the street children. The same thing happened in Jos, Nigeria. Often those who got involved were missionary wives or women who, until this point, had not seen the potential or possibility of this kind of ministry.

More recently, SIM's outreach has gone another step forward: we are consulting with other mission agencies who are experts in the area of children's ministries. We presently have a dialogue going with Compassion International. Their head administrator addressed the head administration of SIM about possibilities in children's ministries. Through this dialogue, SIM began to consider ways in which we could affect the thinking of the SIM-related national church leaders throughout the world.

In December 1996 the church leaders of all the SIM-related churches around the world will meet in Addis Ababa, Ethiopia. Compassion International will conduct a day-long seminar to discuss with national church leaders how the church can minister to children on their city streets.

SIM has a strong conviction about the importance of getting the national church involved in meeting the needs of their children. As a mission agency, SIM can act as a broker between the agencies who have expertise and the national churches who are within our influence. We are persuaded that bringing these two groups together is extremely significant.

How have our new policy and strategies to include children in our ministries affected our concerns for outreach to Muslims? Let me share a recent fax from Jos, Nigeria:

> We are burdened for the Muslim street children in Jos. I guess my burden for these kids started soon after we arrived. I go grocery shopping on Amadu Bello Way every Monday. Each time I see the same boys. They are dressed shabbily and always look hungry. There was one boy who would follow me from one shop to another—quite a distance in most cases. We had a friendship although we never spoke. One day he disappeared and I never saw him again. I don't know if he fell sick or moved to a different place with his Malam.
>
> After meeting this child, I attended a seminar by Dr. Berty on Muslim evangelism. One speaker was a Muslim convert to Christianity. He spoke for a long time about when he was a small boy forced to beg on the streets. He talked about the abuses and how hungry he was much of the time. Sometimes he needed medical attention and no one helped him.
>
> During this seminar, I felt God leading me to do something for these boys in Jos. I talked to Leslie who is working with the prostitutes; she also has a burden for the street children. We began to brainstorm and decided to start a meeting with the kids. At the end of our first five weeks, after

beginning to gain the children's trust and friend-
ship, we had grown from 14 to 54 children. We
feed the children and tell them Bible stories.

This week a seven-year-old boy, Shemu, attended
the meeting. He looked very thin and weak. If all
I can do is feed Shemu and he learns that we
care about him, I am somewhat content.

As a friend said, "We want to plant the seed of
faith in their hearts." *I pray that the Lord will use
our contact with these little children to be a major
breakthrough for the gospel.*

We have no idea where our commitment to children's
ministry will take us, but we do know that SIM is growing—
both numerically and spiritually—through this new focus. Our
outreach to children can be a tool that enables SIM to reach
her "church-planting" goals in a far greater way than we ever
expected. As we encourage local churches to take up the ban-
ner of care and concern for needy children, their ministry will
prove to be infinitely more important than anything we as a
mission society can do for the children.

For SIM, we have no option; ministry to children must
continue to be vital to our outreach and church-planting goals.
We certainly have no regrets concerning our decision to integrate children's ministry into our mission philosophy. The resulting blessings have been just as much ours as the children's.

11

The Church and the World's Children

Sam Martin

"Let the little children to come to Me, and do not forbid them; for of such is the kingdom of God" (Mark 10:14 NKJ).

As a student studying theology and preparing for full-time pastoral ministry, the importance of reaching children and young people with the good news of Jesus Christ was impressed upon me. Studies and research done by ministries working primarily through church Sunday schools indicated that in Great Britain and North America the majority of people who professed to be Christians accepted Christ as Savior and Lord between the ages of 4 and 14 years.

Such results and research gave birth to ministerial training institutions, such as Bible schools and theological colleges, to courses and programs specifically designed to train and prepare young men and women to work in the area of youth and children's ministries. In turn these programs gave birth to positions within church ministries and para-church ministries to full-time staff with the title "Youth Pastor" or "Children's Pastor." Without a doubt this period was an exciting time for the church of Jesus Christ, but in most instances such positions were a luxury too many churches could not afford and, globally, it seemed to make little impact. Reaching children and young people through specialized ministries began really as a North American concept and gradually found its way into other developed countries such as those in Great Britain.

However, let me say again—globally, there has been little impact. Today more than one-third of the world's population, that is, some 1.8 billion people are under the age of 15. It is estimated that 80–85 percent of these youngsters live in what was referred to for years as the "Third World" and today as the "Two-Thirds World." Behind these statistics we find the faces of children: children of the world's slums; children of the night; street children. These children struggle for survival and are exploited at every turn for cheap labor or sex, sometimes both. They are rejected, forgotten and often thrown out with the garbage. Behind these statistics we find those whom Jesus spoke about when he said, "Suffer the children to come to me . . . ." These are children whom the Lord Jesus not only loves but for whom he died!

As a human being I am moved by the state of the world's children. As an evangelical Christian I am disturbed. As a mission leader I am challenged. As a pastor I am ashamed, because it seems no one cares, and that as far as the church is concerned children and youth beyond our geographical boundary do not matter. Perhaps it is a case of "out of sight, out of mind." Yet from a biblical perspective we must do something, and from the perspective of evangelical Christianity we cannot ignore those who make up perhaps the largest "unreached people group" in the world—children! Yes, globally, children need Jesus Christ.

Of the world's under-15 population, over 1.4 billion are growing up in non-Christian homes or in areas and countries where little if any outreach focuses on them. The world's children present the church with perhaps its greatest challenge and greatest opportunity. Jesus' statement " the harvest truly is great, but the labourers are few . . ." is sadly true today of the world's children. This needy unreached people group is growing daily—on cold lonely streets, on city garbage dumps, in refugee camps. Perhaps more than any other group in the world, these youngsters need to both hear and experience the love of God. But for that to happen, things need to change.

It may be, of course, that what I have said and what I am seeking to convey could be challenged. So let me at this juncture ask you to consider whether the following statements are not true in your situation and in the church world:

- The missions budget of the local church does not include support for a ministry with a clear mandate to reach the world's children, this great unreached group.

- Generally speaking, mission outreach focuses on the needs of adults. We send adults to reach adults and if children are reached that is a bonus.

- Today we have "specialists" working as children's pastors and youth pastors in our local churches and through national para-church ministries, but we rarely find such workers when it comes to what we call "the foreign mission field."

- The church looks at the world through "adult eyes."

- Mission support and interest today lie not with young adults but with senior adults.

If we have neglected the world's children, as I suggest we not only have but are continuing to do, I believe there is still hope! With repentant hearts we need to realize that the Great Commission of Christ to go into all the world with the gospel, often referred to as "the supreme task of the church," **includes the world of children!** Such a realization should lead us as the church, the body of Christ, to seek three vital, necessary things. If we are going to reach this forgotten yet precious group of people, the world's children, we need to seek

- the spirit of conviction,
- the spirit of compassion to fulfill the task and
- the spirit of commitment to complete the task.

Obviously it is important that we understand each of these statements, so let us consider each in turn, praying that God's Spirit will speak to us as we do so.

THE SPIRIT OF CONVICTION CONCERNING THE TASK

Basically we must ask ourselves, "Does the task defined as the Great Commission, based on Matthew 28, include going into the world of children? Or, to put it simply, "Do children need to hear? Do they have a right to hear the gospel of Jesus Christ?"

Unless we are convinced that children need to be reached, the gospel is not just for adults and children matter to God, a great company of people will never be reached. If we accept the Bible as our source, we will have a spirit of conviction regarding ministry to children. From a theological and biblical perspective, my conviction is that children are definitely included in the task of reaching the world with the gospel. From my limited experience of working with glue-sniffing orphans and those struggling for survival on city dumps—children in countries such as Haiti, Guatemala and Kenya—I am convinced the only hope children have is the gospel of Jesus Christ!

Consider the following Scriptures and truths:

- Jesus had time for children: "And He took them [the children] up in His arms, . . . and blessed them" (Mark 10:16 NKJ).

- Jesus was upset when the disciples sought to keep the children from him: "But when Jesus saw it, He was greatly displeased . . ." (Mark 10:14 NKJ).

- Jesus gave a strong warning to those who would cause a child to stumble: "It would be better for him . . . if he were drowned in the depth of the sea" (Matthew 18:6 NKJ).

- Jesus identified with the children: "Whoever receives one of these little children . . . receives Me . . ." (Mark 9:37 NKJ).

Dr. J. Vernon McGee, commenting on Mark 10:16 says, "Our Lord took the children in his arms, put his hands on them and blessed them. He never did take anybody else up in his arms like that!"[1] Surely as one considers the example of Christ, one experiences the spirit of conviction with regard to the gospel and children. Of course it is important to remember that the Good News of Jesus Christ, the gospel, can be summarized by four simple statements, four basic truths.

1. God loves.
2. God cares and understands.
3. God heals and forgives.
4. God has a plan.

Who needs to hear this truth more than children in the developing world? When you are alone, rejected by family and friends and forgotten by society, how important to be told that there is a God who loves you! When life is all messed up; when sniffing glue becomes a way to escape the pains of hunger and stealing a way to survive; when selling your body is a false but easy way to find some kind of love and affection; and when you are too embarrassed to look anyone in the eye, how necessary it is to discover a God who not only loves but who also cares and understands. When stealing and prostitution and all that goes with such activities have marred you for life, how good to know that this loving, caring God understands enough to heal and forgive! When life is all yesterdays, with no tomorrows, it is thrilling to be given hope because God has a plan— a plan to give the lowliest child a future and hope.

We, as individuals and as the church, need to rediscover with passion the conviction that Jesus Christ is the answer and the gospel is for children as well as adults because then, and only then, will we be convicted about the task.

THE SPIRIT OF COMPASSION TO FULFILL THE TASK

Being convinced and convicted about the "task," that is, the fact that the Great Commission includes children, is but the first step. The second step is to rediscover the spirit of compassion to fulfill the task. Again we must consider the example of our Lord and Savior Jesus Christ, who truly was and is the Spirit of Compassion. Consider these examples drawn from the Scriptures. (In each example the emphasis is added.)

- "But when He saw the multitudes, He was moved with **compassion** for them, because they were weary and scattered, like sheep having no shepherd" (Matthew 9:36 NKJ).

- "And when Jesus went out He saw a great multitude; and He was moved with **compassion** for them, and healed their sick" (Matthew 14:14 NKJ).

- "Then Jesus called His disciples to Him and said, 'I have **compassion** on the multitude, because they have continued with Me three days and have nothing to eat. And I do not want to send them away hungry . . .'" (Matthew 15:32 NKJ).

- "So Jesus had **compassion** and touched their eyes" (Matthew 20:34a NKJ).

The New Testament gives many additional examples of the compassion of Christ, but we need to be reminded of two things: the source of compassion and the challenge of compassion. In 2 Corinthians 1:3 we read, "Praise be to the God and Father of our Lord Jesus Christ, the Father of **compassion** and the God of all comfort . . . ." The source of compassion is God Himself. In Colossians 3:12 we find the challenging words of Paul: "Therefore, as God's chosen people, holy and dearly beloved, clothe yourselves with **compassion** . . . ."

Sometime ago I read a statement that went something like this, "Almost everyone pities children, but only a few have compassion for children." When considered, this comment seems to be fair on the position the average church takes to the needs of the world's children. Pity they have but little compassion. This, of course, raises the question, "Are pity and compassion not the same?" The dictionary defines pity and compassion as follows:

Pity: A feeling of sorrow for another person's sorrow.

Compassion: A feeling of pity that makes one want to help or show mercy.

Pity looks, sees and feels but stops there. Compassion looks, sees, feels and then does something! Matthew 20:34 (NKJ) illustrates this idea: "So Jesus had compassion and touched their eyes." Pity sees; compassion touches.

Too often over the years, as I have visited areas where needy children are struggling to survive, I heard the words, "Many have come to look at us, to see the conditions. They promised to help, but they never came back." These visitors proffered pity but engaged in little if any real compassion.

Jesus' example opens to us the challenge of doing something—of helping by reaching out and in practical ways demonstrating the love of Christ through touch. But what do we do? And how do we do it?

Following are some practical suggestions that require examination of the mission policy statement and philosophy of the church. These ideas, given as questions, also promote discussions with mission agencies and boards being supported by the church to determine the place of children in ministry outreach.

- Who is going to reach the world's children for Christ?
- How best can the gospel be presented to such needy children?
- How can we educate today's Christians to the needs of children?
- What can we do as a local church to meet such needs?
- How does our mission budget reflect God's concern for children?
- To an adult perspective, how biased is our world mission view?
- What place do women, the mothers of tomorrow in developing countries, have in our mission thinking?
- What can we do to influence government foreign policy with respect to children?

In some ways, compassion gives life and conviction to the words of Jesus and presents a constant challenge. Take, for example, the words from Matthew 15:32 (NKJ), previously quoted: "I have compassion, . . . I do not want to send them away hungry, lest they faint on the way." Today, even as you read this, approximately 100,000 children will die from malnutrition and related illness. Today, many are hungry and fainting all around us. Compassion can make the difference. K. G. McMillan made a comment on one occasion that presents this fact in another light: *The difference between an ordinary Christian and a deeply committed one is that the ordinary Christian gets emotional while the deeply committed Christian gets involved.* We need the spirit of conviction to understand the task and the spirit of compassion to fulfill that task. Conviction without compassion is like faith without works. Conviction enables us to see the need and convinces us about the biblical truth concerning the need. Compassion puts feet to our faith, causing belief to become action!

COMMITMENT TO THE TASK

Mr. Tetsunao Yamamori, president of Food for the Hungry, states, "Unless a profound and dramatic change in our global evangelization takes place, the huge mass of unsaved humanity will grow even larger."[2]

The truth is, more non-Christians live on the earth now than at any time since the world began, and no one would argue with the fact that the majority of them are under 15 years of age. This reality calls into question the entire missionary program of today's church. With all our resources, manpower, finances and technology, why are we falling behind?

There are, no doubt, many answers, but let me suggest that the primary reason for what is happening is spiritual. Today a spiritual problem exists among believers in evangelical churches. The problem can be summed up in a few simple words: Many Christians today are not committed to the gospel nor to the biblical injunction to go into all the world with the gospel. If conviction is dependent upon compassion, then compassion is dependent upon commitment.

In the early 1900s, conferences were held in both Great Britain and the United States to discuss and debate the problems then being faced by churches and mission agencies in relation to missions in general. Out of such discussion came papers published in book form by Andrew Murray. In one such paper pertaining to the history of the Church Missionary Society, Murray records the following statement from the report: "We have learned in our long survey that *missionary advance depends upon spiritual life* . . . . Consecration and the evangelization of the world go together. . . . *Seek the deepening of the spiritual life, and missionary consecration will follow.*"[3]

It is clear that the problems being faced today by missiologists, mission agencies and church leaders can be traced back to a spiritual problem. The dilemma is nothing less than a lack of commitment to Jesus Christ.

Therefore, the greatest need is to call Christian people—the body of Christ—to a fresh and sincere commitment to the

117

Lord Jesus Christ. Yes, we must experience conviction concerning the task, and we need the spirit of compassion if we are going to fulfill the task. But both are dependent upon commitment—commitment not so much to the task as to the Lord of the task. This means the surrender of all we have and are to Christ and the gospel. On his fifty-ninth birthday, years after he began his work and entered into service in Africa, Dr. David Livingston, one of the greatest pioneer missionaries of all time, wrote in his diary: *My Jesus, my King, my life, my all. I again dedicate my whole self to Thee. Accept me and grant that ere this year is gone I may finish my task.* Such a prayer of commitment must be on the lips of today's Christians if we are to reach the world for Christ, and that includes the world of children!

In conclusion

Two further priorities must be mentioned because the task is far greater than the resources of the developed world and, thus, must be shared by churches all over the world.

The first priority lies with the national church in each needy area. This insight has been brought home to me from two specific sources: my local church and my overseas experience.

My local church has a heart for God unmatched anywhere in North America. (Of course, I am somewhat biased.) Deeply committed to missions at home and overseas, we are an active sending church, a giving church and a praying church. Located some thirty miles east of the city of Toronto, we have, for a number of years, sponsored a "breakfast club" in one of the roughest, toughest environments, known as "Jane-Finch." We supply breakfast food, share in special occasions and provide clothing and other items for the children. We are happy to do so in the name of Christ and will continue to do so as long as we are able. However, sometimes I wonder why a church some 30 miles away has to do the job. We pass literally hundreds of churches to reach our little mission field of needy children. Would it not be more natural and feasible for a local church to fill this need? The answer would be yes, but the fact is, *we* have to do it!

My work overseas also impressed upon me the necessity for the church in the local area to take action. For example, I met a young man in The Dominican Republic who, with his family, became burdened for needy children on the outskirts of Santo Domingo. The couple felt God leading them to begin a school and feeding center. They approached their home church, a Bible-believing, totally evangelical church for help and were refused. The church was anticipating a building program so monies were not available.

The young man became so discouraged he gave up on the church and on Christ. Thank God, when The Arms of Jesus Children's Mission came alongside and began to support this work, the young man came back to Christ.

I became aware of this local-church-involvement principle again when I was exposed to the filth, poverty and desperate needs of children living on a dump in Central America. On seeing the need, I asked the workers what their church or other local churches were doing to help. The reply came, "They don't want to know. Even the pastors refuse to come and see."

Surely Christians and churches closest to the need ought to be the first to respond. The task is not the sole responsibility of those from the developing world—we can help and we will help—but the local church must do its job.

- If the national church does not care about its own, is it fair to expect the international church to care?
- It is more practical: although there must be partnership.
- It is certainly much more in accord with the Scriptures because the locally needy area is the "Jerusalem" of the local church.

The second priority is the truth that needy children are the largest unreached group today. Ironically while working on this chapter, I noticed an ad in the October 2, 1995 edition of *Christianity Today*, that went something like this (names have been changed):

> <u>Minister to Children</u>. Second Baptist Church of Mid Hurst, Arizona, seeks full-time staff member with vision and administrative skills to develop a growing children's ministry. Growing church has 1500 in worship and 1,000 children involved in various ministry programs and over 200 adults committed to children's ministry.

This ad represents a positive move by that church, although it is somewhat revealing that only 13.3 percent of worshiping adults are committed to the children's ministry.

Let me remind you that 1.4 billion children living in the developing world are in desperate need of the gospel of Jesus Christ. Global 2000, one of the most respected documents which predicts the state of the world in the year 2000, forecasts a world that will be more crowded, more polluted and more vulnerable to all kinds of disturbances than today's world. This prediction means that the number of suffering children will increase, therefore, the need will increase and the challenge facing the church will increase. Clearly if we reach today's children, the world has more hope for tomorrow!

Mark 10:13 states, "And they were bringing children to him, that he might touch them. . . ." May it become true of our generation, and **may it be said of the church at the end of the century that** "they brought children to Jesus."

NOTES

[1] J. Vernon McGee, *Through the Bible Vol. IV*, Bible Commentary (Thomas Nelson Publishers, 1983), p. 6.

[2] Tetsunao Yamamori, *God's New Envoys* (Multnomah Press, Portland, OR, 1987), p. 10.

[3] Andrew Murray, *Key to the Missionary Problem* (Christian Literature Crusade, 1979), pp. 80–86.

Part 3

Strategies and Opportunities

12

The 4/14 Window: Child Ministries and Mission Strategy

Dan Brewster

Cutting-edge mission groups today are making some of the most significant advances in the history of Christianity by looking closely at the 10/40 window. Here live most of the remaining people groups who have never had opportunity to hear the gospel. The concepts of the 10/40 window and people groups are among the most important innovations in missions thinking in generations. These two principles have enabled mission leaders to focus evangelism efforts in ways never before possible.

Another window, within the window, however, may be just as significant, and may enable many frontier mission efforts to be even more effective. I call that window the 4/14 window.

WHY THE 4/14 WINDOW?

In 1992 Dr. Bryant Myers, director of World Vision's MARC division, made an eye-opening presentation to the EFMA

125

Executive Retreat. His paper[1] painted a sobering picture of the numbers and conditions of children and youth throughout the world and noted some of the implications that this huge and often suffering people group presents to mission strategists today. He presented a stunning graphic (below) showing that in the U.S.A. nearly 85 percent of people who make a decision for Christ, do so between the ages of 4 and 14.

The extent to which these data hold true for populations outside the U.S.A. is unclear, though there is much to suggest that they do. At the very least, however, they confirm evidence that children and young people are indeed "the world's most fruitful field."

Figure 12:1
Ages at which people become Christians

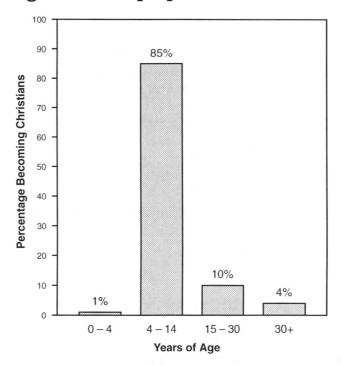

Years of Age

Each time I have shared the data on this graph, I have conducted my own survey among 4–14-year-olds. My exercise has largely confirmed this incredible missiological fact, although my informal results have yielded a somewhat lower figure than Dr. Myers'—generally about 60 percent to his 85 percent.

CHILDREN AS A PEOPLE GROUP

The category "children" is, of course, much too broad to fit the normal definitions of a people group. People groups are typically defined along ethnic, geographic, habitat or social affinity lines. But such delineations have a distinct adult bias. Many distinct groups of children and young people warrant not only ministry to address their physical needs but also the attention of missiologists in development of effective mission strategies. Strategic consideration should be given, for example, to the children who have migrated to cities in search of employment or education. In the 4/14 window many children in such situations provide gateways to their people. Unfortunately, adequate attention to these groups has yet to materialize among mission strategists.

An enormous people group
The number of children in the world is reason to make us concerned about their state. Over one-third of the world's population, 1.8 billion children, are under the age of 15. One and a half billion of them—almost 85 percent—live in the Two Thirds World.

Dr. Myers used another remarkable graphic (next page) to illustrate these facts. It shows the composition of developing world societies and the astonishing fact of the huge proportion of the populations of those societies who are less than 15 years of age.[2]

Figure 12:2
Adolescents aged 10–19

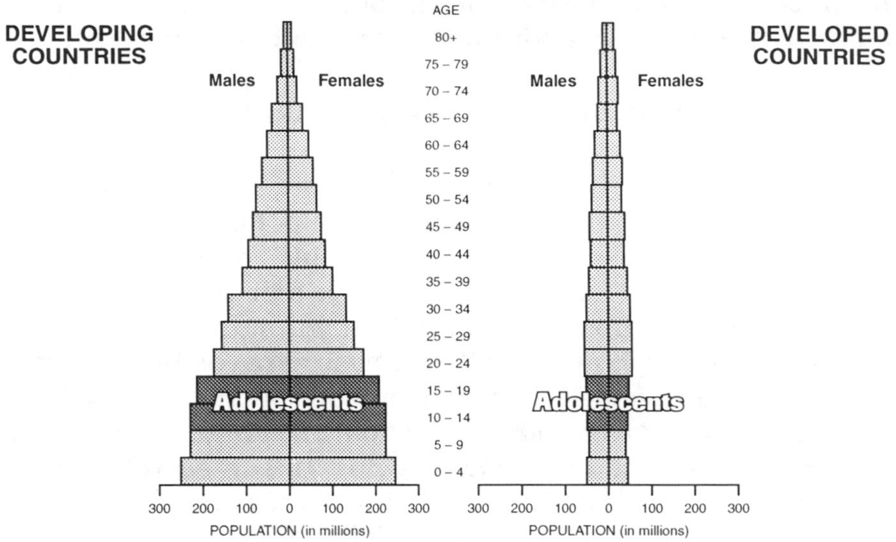

DEVELOPING COUNTRIES

Males Females

DEVELOPED COUNTRIES

Males Females

AGE

80+
75 – 79
70 – 74
65 – 69
60 – 64
55 – 59
50 – 54
45 – 49
40 – 44
35 – 39
30 – 34
25 – 29
20 – 24
15 – 19
10 – 14
5 – 9
0 – 4

Adolescents

Adolescents

300 200 100 0 100 200 300
POPULATION (in millions)

300 200 100 0 100 200 300
POPULATION (in millions)

A receptive people group

Missiologists also document the reasons for apparent changes in receptivity to the gospel. The School of World Mission's shelves at Fuller Seminary are brimming with theses and dissertations exploring the reasons for resistance and receptivity. One clear and consistent factor is that people tend to be receptive when their lives are disrupted. The poor and exploited tend to be much more receptive to the gospel than those with means. No people group today has lives more disrupted by poverty and exploitation than those of children and youth.

Any review of the conditions of the world's children confirm that children are suffering, unwanted and victimized.

Suffering

For years we were told that some 40,000 children die around the world *every day,* many of them from malnutrition

and preventable diseases. Thankfully, UNICEF has now reduced the annual childhood death figure to *only* 35,000 per
day.[3]

UNICEF's *State of the World's Children 1995* indicates
that considerable progress has been made in dealing with many
childhood diseases over the last three years.

> Malnutrition has been reduced; immunization
> levels are generally being maintained or in-
> creased; measles deaths are down by 80 percent
> compared to pre-immunization levels; large ar-
> eas of the developing world, including all of the
> western hemisphere, have become free of polio;
> iodine deficiency disorders are being eliminated
> . . . . Such progress means that approximately
> 2.5 million fewer children will die in 1996 than
> in 1990 . . . . And it means that at least three-
> quarters of a million fewer children each year will
> be disabled, blinded, crippled or mentally re-
> tarded.[4]

Nevertheless, many challenges remain and children in
many countries still face enormous risks. Those in the 4/14
window remain the most affected and vulnerable group for
every kind of disease and suffering.

Unwanted

We know that very many of these children are still unwanted, evidenced by the appallingly high rates of abortion,
especially in the so-called developed nations.

An equally shocking and growing problem is the number of street children around the world. In August last year I
saw firsthand the horror of the street children problem in Sao
Paulo, Brazil. I noted the following in my personal diary:

> *Family abuse is extremely common here in Sao*
> *Paulo. There were 42,000 cases of abuse reported*

129

in Sao Paulo in a three-year period of time. Only 10 percent or less of abuse cases are reported which means there were nearly one-half million such cases. Many children in Brazil die of malnutrition, but many more die because they're on drugs and therefore don't eat. They die of malnutrition, but the real cause is drug addiction.

Actually, visiting where the children live was like a descent into hell . . . .

We followed the leader over the railing of the bridge, hanging out over the street then slithering down a steep slope to get close so he could peek in a couple of cracks and see who was there. He told us to wait: apparently they were having sex . . . . The counselor (pastor) had a talk with the youngsters, and they invited us in. They helped us crawl through a little hole and drop down into their cave-like area beneath the bridge.

The place was unimaginably foul, the smell of urine and feces powerful. The young people had some blankets and a few possessions laid out. The amazing and beautiful thing was the relationship Suzanne Holanda, director of JEAME, has with the kids. She hugged them and talked with them, and we gathered around and prayed together.

We listened to the young people talk about harassment by the police and about their friends who are being beaten by the police . . . . We visited with these kids for half an hour, then climbed back out to the hole and onto the street below.

Victimized

We all know these are not the only problems children face. My exposure to the suffering of children during the Rwanda war was far too up-close and personal for my comfort. In three trips to Rwanda during and following the war, I personally saw countless children with limbs cut off, wounds and scars too ghastly to describe and, invariably, horror stories of mistreatment, torture and abuse.

What happened in Rwanda in 1994 is doubtless the worst such tragedy in recent history, but sadly it is not the only place where children are victimized. Indeed, it is now clear that the very nature of warfare is changing. UNICEF notes that

> at one time wars were fought between armies; but in the wars of the last decade far more children than soldiers have been killed and disabled. Over that period, approximately 2 million children have died in wars, between 4 and 5 million have been physically disabled, more than 5 million have been forced into refugee camps and more than 12 million have been left homeless.[5]

The needs and injustices behind such shocking statistics cry out for attention. But the net result globally is a suffering, disrupted people group which is often hungry for the touch of the gospel in their lives. Increasing numbers of traumatized children surely present significant ministry opportunities and challenges. Attention to this 4/14 window is, I believe, imperative for any mission agency serious about reaching truly receptive people in any other "window" of the world.

A FORGOTTEN PEOPLE GROUP

In light of all these factors, the relative lack of attention mission agencies give to children's ministries is curious. What do we have to say, from a missiological standpoint, to the poorest, most numerous, most disrupted, most hurting and possibly most receptive of the world's population groups?

Sadly, not much.

Overlooked in our strategy planning

At the GCOWE 95 consultation held in Seoul, Korea, the "How do we get there?" section of the planning workbooks suggested the consideration of the needs of children and youth. And yes, several of the tracks could be said to have related peripherally to children and youth. Obviously there are many millions of Chinese children, Muslim children, urban children and the like. But none of the tracks nor any of the main plenary or workshop sessions were specifically devoted to children.[6]

Overlooked in missions literature

Similarly missions journals show a paucity of articles relating to reaching this most receptive group. A colleague of mine, Gordon Mullenix, has searched the back issues of *Evangelical Missions Quarterly* and *Missiology* for articles on children and mission strategy. What literature exists is primarily of the how-to variety. Material on Christian education, curriculum design and Sunday school programs receive attention, but strategic analysis is missing. The number of articles specifically on the subject of children and missions can probably be counted on both hands with a few fingers change.

There are a couple of notable exceptions. One is Wolfe Hansen's article, "Young People in Young Nations—Strategic Objective" (EMQ II: Summer 1966), in which he suggested that "the time has come to make the younger generation our prime objective in evangelism. To neglect it," Wolfe says, "would be a strategic blunder. Winning young people must be made a definite goal and be given priority in our plans."

That observation, stated almost 30 years ago, is still true but has not been given priority in our plans.

Another of the few articles on child ministries is Jim Reapsome's "Editor's Analysis: Where do kids fit in mission priorities?" (EMQ 22/3: July 1985). In this editorial, Reapsome asks, "Are [children] being slighted by more majestic issues, by more serious concerns? Do we, subconsciously perhaps, look down our noses at agencies that work with children?" The answer to that question may be "yes."

THE 4/14 WINDOW
AND SOCIAL ACTION

The Great Commandment is as valid as the Great Commission. Yet the adult bias that tends to overlook children in furthering the Great Commission is common among relief and development agencies as well. This preference prevails in spite of child survival programs which many agencies use and which attract so much government funding.

UNICEF research consistently indicates that *the* most significant interventions for *national* development are child health and education.[7]

Again, Compassion's experience bears out this concept. We do not say we do community development, and our funds do not assist in broad community development activities. But our child development projects, if well designed and managed, often result in better quality community development outcomes. We have found that communities can often unite around the needs of their children even though other issues are divisive. Parents will join together to make improvements to schools, water supplies and roads as a response to the challenges of their children. Thus, even if agencies set goals for doing national or community development, many would do well to look more closely at ministry to children.

CHILDREN AS COMMUNITY HEALTH AND EDUCATION RESOURCES

National development strategies should not only look on children as recipients of health and education efforts. They should also view children as effective community health and education resources. The Child-to-Child Trust initiatives around the world recognize the role children play in dissemination of information. Children often have major responsibility for the care of their younger siblings.

> We know someone who is a teacher and health worker. She looks after two children. One is four and one is two. She keeps them safe . . . . She helps them when they are sick . . . . She helps them to grow up healthy . . . .

> Who is this teacher who does so much for her pupils and does it so well? She is their elder sister—and she is eleven years old.[8]

Many development practitioners know that children play an important role in promoting change and are sources of useful information. David Drucker illustrates:

> Our Jeep bumps along to a stop in a fairly isolated village. While I am talking to the village midwife, three or four hundred children, some carrying smaller ones, come to stare at me, the foreigner. I notice the doctor going among the children looking at their arms . . . . [He] tells me that he is taking this opportunity to check the immunization status of the children by looking for scars on their arms. "How long will it take you?" I ask.

134

"Perhaps 45 minutes," he says, "but it is worth taking the time since we are here."

I persuade him to ask the children themselves each to look at the child next to him, and if there is no scar to hold up the arm. Two false starts, while the explanation is clarified and soon . . . with a buzz of curiosity and excitement [they] inspect each other. I say to the doctor, "From beginning to end the activity took four minutes and now we have 40 minutes saved to tell why we are looking [and] why it is important . . . ." I add, "None of these children have had any special education or spent seven years at medical school. Yet they are the experts—experts at standing next to other children and inspecting their arms."[9]

THE 4/14 WINDOW AND LEADERSHIP DEVELOPMENT

Frontier mission agencies have done all of us a great service in focusing our attention on AD 2000 and Beyond. However, while few have omitted the "Beyond" in their labels, the heavy emphasis has always been on the AD 2000. (I am personally pleased, though, to see David Barrett's *AD 2000 Global Monitor* is now *AD 2025 Global Monitor*.) While I enthusiastically support all efforts to evangelize the world by AD 2000, I also applaud the longer-range view. In the push to meet the AD 2000 "deadline," some Christians may have assumed we don't have time to wait for young Christians to mature into their place of leadership. Looking toward AD 2000 *and beyond* affirms that we can still afford to *grow* the church.

What are our strategies for *growing* the leadership needed to lead the churches in 2025? A final example from our experience in Compassion suggests the potential of this approach. We were interested when Mr. Gene Davis, a researcher for the Unreached People's Clearinghouse, told how significant our programs were in developing the leadership for the church in India. He recounted how at least 17 of our formerly sponsored children were among the evangelists who have accounted for over 6,000 people coming to Christ in a formerly unreached group. A patient approach to ministry in the 4/14 window has apparently resulted in a substantial people movement among adults—in the 10/40 window.

Certain distinctives in Compassion's ministry make this kind of spin-off benefit possible. Among them are—

- Deliberately, exclusively and effectively working with children *through churches,* thereby helping them catch the vision for ministry to children and equipping them to do so.

- Working with *individual* children to ensure that each one has adequate opportunity to hear and respond to the gospel.

- Staying long enough to make a difference and give time for genuine Christian maturity to emerge.

Parents know it takes at least 18 years to "develop" their children. We realize that child development is a long-term proposition. But the long-term commitment, as was discovered in India and elsewhere, results in many of the children receiving enough Christian training to equip them to be serious Christian leaders.

THE 4/14 WINDOW AND UNREACHED PEOPLES

There is even much potential for reaching into unreached people areas through a strategy of focusing on meeting the needs of this most vulnerable part of virtually every people group. Dr. Danny Martin of Missions to the Unreached, now based in Singapore, told me that he would like nothing better than to have child assistance programs in each of his new churches along the southern Chinese rim. Such ministries, he says, would help consolidate and solidify the new young churches and provide a strong foundation for further church growth and outreach. More recently, missionaries working in Mongolia and other parts of China have told me the same thing. A variety of child-focused ministries could constitute a "second wave" of reinforcements for these pioneer church planters.

THE 4/14 WINDOW AND MISSION PRIORITIES

The most effective mission groups today are interested in getting into the 10/40 window. Many such groups may find the 4–14 age group—the window within the window—to be one of the "doors" to that window. Initially, missions involved with the CoMission in the former Soviet Union found this concept true. The 4/14 window can also, of course, be key to more effective ministry to parents of that age group and other adults. But just as importantly, ministry in the 4/14 window is productive and fruitful for its own sake and for the sake of developing the Christian leadership we need for the future.

WHAT SHALL WE DO? (ACTS 2:37)

The plight of children around the world is well known to most of us, though perhaps most of us do not take time to reflect on their needs. Clearly missions, churches and development agencies must deliberately include children in any efforts to relieve human suffering and become more aggressive advocates for alleviating the suffering and exploitation of children. From a kingdom perspective, though, it is just as important for mission agencies to consider carefully the spiritual needs of children and young people, and the potential of such ministries, for fulfilling the Great Commission.

At the very least, we must agree that we cannot ignore the 4/14 window. Ignore the children now and we'll have more difficulty reaching them later. We also must not assume that taking children and youth seriously is only someone else's mission. Clearly, deliberate mission to children and youth represents a great potential for many mission organizations.

Finally, we should look for ways to cooperate in more effective outreaches to children and youth. The call to "Celebrate the Child" in 1997 [see information on the page following this chapter] by representatives of various child and youth ministries is one promising initiative. We might also participate together in consultations in which we explore ways, for example, to pilot test initiatives in Unreached Peoples' areas. Joint partnerships in which we share vision, resources and responsibilities in forms of youth ministries may also be possible for some groups and in some areas.

Let's take a closer look through this window within a window.

QUESTIONS FOR DISCUSSION

- What are the implications of the 4/14 window for mission strategizing? What are the implications for your mission?

- Is there an adult bias in our "usual" mission strategizing? If so, is that a problem?

- What are our strategies for "growing" Christian leaders for the next generation?

- What is your experience in relating child ministries to church planting and growth?

- What is your experience in child ministry as a door opener in unreached peoples initiatives?

- Are seminaries equipping and challenging students with the potential of child ministries?

- What are some ways we can cooperate in new initiatives?

NOTES

[1] Bryant Myers, "The State of the World's Children: A Strategic Challenge to the Christian Mission in the 1990s," paper presented to EFMA Executive Leadership Retreat, Glen Eyrie, September 1992.

[2] Adapted from T. Merrick, "World Population in Transition," *World Population Bulletin,* April 1986. Cited in "The State of the World's Children: A Strategic Challenge to the Christian Mission in the 1990s," by Bryant Myers.

[3] *The State of the World's Children,* UNICEF (Oxford University Press, 1994).

[4] *The State of the World's Children,* UNICEF (Oxford Press, 1995), pp. 12, 13.

[5] Ibid, p. 2.

[6] GCOWE 95, the AD 2000 and Beyond Movement Participants Book, May 1995.

[7] See, for example, "The Child in South Asia, Issues in Development as if Children Mattered," (New Delhi: UNICEF, 1988). Also see "World Declaration on the Survival, Protection and Development of Children" (World Summit for Children, UNICEF, 1990).

[8] Audrey Aaron, Hugh Hawes, Juliet Gayton; *Child-to-Child* (London: The Macmillan Press, Ltd., 1979), p. 6.

[9] David Drucker, "Ask a Silly Question, Get a Silly Answer—Community Participation and the Demystification of Health Care," in *Community Management: Asian Experience and Perspectives,* David C. Korten, ed. (West Hartford CT: Kumarian Press, 1986), p. 163.

Declaration

In response to the commission of our Lord Jesus Christ, we the under-
signed declare that we will **Celebrate the Child** during 1997–98! In support
of this declaration, we affirm:

1. Childrens ministry is equally important as ministry to youth and adults.
2. The task of ministry to children must include evangelism and discipleship.
3. Any viable ministry to children must involve the family.
4. Children must be integrated into a nurturing community of believers.
5. The gifts of children themselves must be celebrated and expressed.

By using this theme and logo wherever possible, we covenant to make a
concerted effort in our ministries to emphasize the vital importance of
ministry with children.

Several denominations and Christian organizations
are cooperating in this effort. Interested parties
should contact the:

> Institute of Evangelism
> Billy Graham Center
> 500 East College Avenue
> Wheaton, IL 60187
> (630) 752-5904 (Area code effective Aug 96)

13

A Cry from the Inner City: Don't Throw Them Away

Bill Wilson

America refuses to face the problem that unless there is a revolution in the basic education of our children, the nation will crumble from within. Demise will not come from economic collapse but from moral bankruptcy that is already well on its way. The conditions I deal with each day in Bushwick, the South Bronx and Harlem are not isolated social phenomena that will become extinct. The same problems are invading "Everytown, U.S.A." like a plague.

To the church I say, "Wake up!" We can no longer ignore what is happening to our children. Why do we place a forty-thousand-dollar price tag on a new BMW and zero value on a child who fails to meet our standards? We can't afford to keep throwing our children away.

A recent news report depicted the tragic results of considering a child to be disposable. When I saw the headline of a final edition of the New York Daily News, I froze. The bold type read "WHO IS SHE?" Beneath those words was a hand-drawn sketch of a young girl with long black hair. Her eyes were dark and haunting, her brow furrowed.

The child's only identity was her morgue case number: M91-5935. She weighed 25 pounds, and her age was determined to be four years. Construction workers discovered the girl along the highway at the edge of Harlem—her severely decomposed body stuffed into a picnic cooler. She was nude. Her hands and feet were bound with a cord, her hair in a ponytail.

Her life and death are a mystery. When found, she had been dead for at least a week, her tiny body curled into a fetal position inside a green garbage bag. New York's chief of detectives, Joseph Borrelli, knew only one thing for certain. "Her face showed an awful lot of misery and suffering for a person who's only lived four years," he said.

"Whose child is this?" I wondered. Once she had been a real person who probably liked to play with dolls and watch cartoons. Now she was another child who had been thrown away, a symbol of the utter despair that hangs like a thick cloud over our nation's ghettos.

For children like this one I came to live in one of America's toughest neighborhoods, the Bushwick/Bedford-Stuyvesant area of Brooklyn in New York City. This area is considered one of the most deprived and crime-ridden in the country. Most four-year-olds living here don't go to school. But they get a daily education about life—and death—just looking out of their bedroom windows.

In this neighborhood, where unemployment is five times the national average, 83 percent of ninth-grade students drop out of school. Children prowl the streets at 12 years, deal guns at 13, sell drugs on the corner at 15. Many don't live to see their 20th birthday.

In this place, called the "war zone" by cabbies who refuse to drive here, life is disposed of as casually as a candy wrapper. The cops patrol in pairs and wear bulletproof vests. Looking down the block you see drug-infested brownstones and tenement houses. Rusty skeletons of vandalized cars languish on vacant lots. Garbage is piled high—broken bottles and dirty vials that once held crack scattered in the rubble. You'll find drugs—crack houses and heroin shooting galleries—illegal guns and prostitution.

142

Every week I visit the dingy apartments of children who are as naturally gifted and talented as any young person you can name. Yet because of their environment and circumstances, an X has been written on their foreheads, saying to the world, "Don't touch. Don't teach. Don't encourage. You're wasting your time."

Metro Ministries, serving in this ghetto, has a different philosophy. We affirm that it is easier to build boys and girls than to repair men and women. Prevention is at the heart of our programs. Granted, this is not an easy task amid the violence and poverty of New York City. However, we believe no child would turn out badly if he or she had even one person who really cared.

Since 1980 Metro Ministries has been in the forefront of reaching America's forgotten inner cities. Located in the former Rheingold brewery, the Metro Church conducts one of America's largest Sunday schools. It has a staff of more than 60 full-time workers and 300 volunteers who visit more than 16,000 children each week. On Saturdays and Sundays the place comes alive! Metro Ministries is committed to changing America . . . one child at a time. Our building and our 50 buses are filled with children by traveling only two and a half miles from our center in the Bushwick section of Brooklyn. But with thousands more children to reach, we pioneered the concept of the Sidewalk Sunday School. This unique idea allows us to conduct Sunday school classes in different parts of the city and to minister seven days a week beyond the confines of a building. Thousands of children's lives are being changed.

Living in a society without values, the children need Christ-centered education that gives an alternative to the life their neighborhood offers. They need someone who really cares; cares enough to visit them in their homes, spend time with them and keep up with their individual needs.

During Sunday school sessions, the children enjoy fun, games, music and lots of loving attention from staff members. They hear Bible lessons that stress the love of God for each of them personally. "God loves you" is the message that comes through in films, animated videos and skits. From the lessons they learn a new set of values: the importance of working hard and doing well in school; respecting teachers and parents; not lying, cheating or stealing; and avoiding drugs and alcohol. Observers are often shocked when we announce it is time to take an offering. I believe, however, that children need to establish a pattern of supporting the Lord's work through giving. The offering is symbolic: we've received everything from food stamps to subway tokens.

One key to the long-term success of our Sunday school is the thousands of home visits that take place all week long. Children are visited from the time they return home from school until the sun goes down. Each bus captain is responsible for his or her kids. With their assistants, they visit the children each week, getting to know them, their friends and their moms. (Few of the children have dads.) Relationships are built, families are helped and lives are changed.

Every week we print eye-catching flyers telling what is going to happen at Sunday school that week. On any given day we are waiting outside elementary schools at dismissal to hand out flyers to more kids. If they are new on a route, we tell them to have their mothers phone the number on the flyers. We'll assign them a bus number and tell them when it will come by to pick them up.

Several times each year we have special days. Every year we give thousands of Christmas stockings to the children where we minister. The stockings are sewn and stuffed by hundreds of women across the nation who believe in the work the Lord is doing at Metro.

One Mother's Day, a gift to the ministry provided a McDonald's hamburger for every child. The McDonald's crew worked extra hours to make 10,016 hamburgers. One little girl, Tiffany, told Carl Keyes, our adult ministry pastor, "I can't wait to get home with my hamburger."

When asked why she said, "I want to give half to my brother. He's never had a McDonald's hamburger before. Isn't this great?"

Tiffany's little brother, Robert, was four. Nine months earlier he had an infection in his brain caused by the AIDS virus. Since then he has not been able to speak or walk. His mother, an intravenous drug user, is now in a government facility on Rikers Island.

When the kids outgrow their interest in an elementary/ junior high Sunday school, they still want to be part of Metro. Life Clubs (Bible study and recreation) are held during the week for teens who get their start with us. More than a thousand are involved weekly.

The Sunday school has also produced a vibrant adult congregation. Many are parents who saw the impact of Christ on their children. More than one thousand attend our service every Sunday morning.

Sadly, we conduct three funerals for every wedding. The people are not dying of old age; the average age of people we bury is twenty-five. The principal cause of death is AIDS, followed by drug-related violence.

The escalating problems of children and youth are not limited to New York City. They mount up in cities all over America. Consider these facts and statistics:

- More than 30 percent of the population lives below the official poverty line.

- Minority children are far more likely to be poor. Forty-five percent of blacks and 39 percent of Hispanic children are living below the poverty line.

- More than 100,000 children are homeless.

- On an average day 135,000 students bring guns to schools.

- More than four million teenagers are alcoholics.

- Alcohol-related accidents are the leading cause of death among teenagers.

- Every year a million girls become pregnant.

- More than 2.5 million adolescents contract a sexually transmitted disease each year.

- More than a million young people are regular users of drugs.

- One out of ten newborns is exposed to one or more illicit drugs in the womb.

God has given some basic principles on how we are to care for those less fortunate than ourselves. Scripture says,

> When you harvest your crops, don't reap the corners of your fields, and don't pick up stray grains of wheat from the ground. It is the same with our grape crop—don't strip every last piece of fruit from the vines, and don't pick up the grapes that fall to the ground. Leave them for the poor and for those traveling through, for I am Jehovah your God (Leviticus 19:9–10).

We may no longer live in small villages, but we still have a responsibility to our neighbors.

The lessons we have learned are not only for Bushwick or Harlem but also for an abandoned generation in all our inner cities. What we do is based on *principles* not *personality*. Jim Davidson, a clinical psychologist from Ashtabula, Ohio closed his practice. He moved to Cleveland where he founded the Heart and Hand ministry based on the principles of Metro Ministries. Today he serves more than 4,000 children.

146

Clay and Barbara Wallace are the directors for Metro Ministries Dallas/Fort Worth. In just three years they are averaging over 3000 kids on 12 sites with three sidewalk trucks. Clay emphasizes teamwork with his staff of 6 and 80 volunteers. They, as we, have found visitation and commitment to be the key.

The same story is repeated in other parts of the world. Within a couple of months the Sunday school in Hackney, England, which is one of the tougher neighborhoods of London, had over 500 children. Several new sidewalk Sunday schools have been started in the Philippines, one of which had over 1000 kids coming within one month. Other sidewalk Sunday schools have begun in Australia, New Zealand, Malaysia, Holland and many other countries around the world. Charisma and flash aren't necessary, but commitment for the long haul is vital.

To hear the children's cries arising from the inner city, however, you must first become aware of the background and ongoing dynamics of inner city life causing their pain and problems.

DEVELOPMENT OF THE GHETTOS

Following World War II, a combination of the economic boom and the automobile helped to create what we call suburbs. In the migration there, however, the poor were left behind. What was the result? The needy, already separated because of position and race, became separated geographically as well. They filled the empty shells of buildings left behind, forming what are now known as the ghettos.

After the race riots of the 1960s, huge government spending programs were thrown at the problems of the ghettos. By the 1980s most Americans realized that federal efforts had been largely ineffective.

We do have deeply entrenched programs that dominate the lives of the poor. Supposedly those in need can turn for help to:

- the educational system.
- the welfare system.
- the criminal justice system.
- the housing authority.
- the food stamp program.
- the medical system.

Experience has proven that no single approach can meet the needs of those in poverty. Tragically, the programs don't work well with each other. Yet these are the institutions we are forced to deal with. Unfortunately, the basic problem that exists in society can also be found in the church. Most groups begin with noble objectives, but over time their goal changes from "How can we help you?" to "How can we stay in existence?"

PROBLEMS IN THE INNER CITY

The urban areas of America—Los Angeles, Miami, Boston and Detroit, to name a few—are experiencing cultural conflicts and racial hatred at an increasing and alarming pace. How can a wound heal when the scab keeps being pulled off? Everyone is looking for or expecting to find quick and easy answers to inner-city problems.

During the riots between blacks and Hasidic Jews in the Crown Heights neighborhood of Brooklyn, Mayor David Dinkins was pelted with bottles and rocks. The crowd cried, "The mayor is not safe here." If he was not safe with the two thousand police who were in the area to support him that day, who is safe?

Inside—outside

People continue to ask, "Bill, why the violence? Why the killings?" First you have to look at the fabric of the community. Every neighborhood has a unique identity and feeling. Whether you are talking about a square mile in Brooklyn or a single high-rise in the Bronx, a neighborhood has its own "insider versus outsider" thinking.

If you live within well-defined boundaries you are an insider. If you're not an insider and it's nighttime you should be looking over your shoulder. During the day it doesn't matter; but after the workday has ended, people in those neighborhoods know who belongs and who doesn't. Outsiders represent the unknown and are immediately under scrutiny.

Unfortunately, the older teenagers become the guardians of the neighborhood. With nothing better to do than hang out on the corner, they try—no matter what the cost—to develop some kind of self-image. Their first attempt at getting recognition might be to spray paint their names on a wall. They may steal a pair of sneakers, just to prove they can do it. If they really want to show their manhood, they might demonstrate how they can keep outsiders out of their neighborhood.

In countless areas every block, every neighborhood and every *barrio* becomes a private fortress. Each person does what is right in his or her own eyes: they call it "taking care of business."

What I have described is one reason many ministries come and go in the inner city. Tackling the problems day after day, a feeling of hopelessness sets in. That same hopeless feeling has caused people to stop painting over graffiti-covered walls. It seems so futile.

A few years ago I wondered why so few people speak up in the community when they see a wrong committed. People keep quiet because they have come to understand who is really in charge: not the police, not the government, not the educational system and not the churches. The streets are ruled by self-appointed neighborhood tough guys who enjoy being "hard rocks," as they are called. This social system breeds frustration, which manifests itself in hate, turf wars, murders and self-indulgences of all types. Because there is no future, the people develop a take-it-now mentality. Today is all they have.

149

Some wonder, "What about the public schools? Couldn't they make a difference?" The public school system has forsaken the children by failing to teach basic values and principles of life.

Classroom crisis

I wish I could tell you that America's finest teachers are begging to be assigned to schools that need them most. But, generally, this is not happening. When *Time* or *Newsweek* features a teacher of the year who is motivating students in some impoverished area, you are reading about the exception, not the rule. I've spent countless hours talking with students, teachers, parents and administrators about what is happening in the classrooms of the inner city. My conclusion is that, for the most part, the elementary schools are providing free babysitting services under the guise of education. Some are nothing more than holding tanks to keep kids off the streets. This may sound harsh, but our schools have almost given up on preparing underprivileged students for the real world.

The hunger factor

We need to take a close look at the health needs of our young people—not just in the ghetto, but across the land. National statistics show that one out of eight children goes to school hungry. Another six million are at risk because of nutritional deficiencies in their diet. It is estimated that half a million American kids are suffering from malnutrition.

I recall talking to the late Mark Buntain, noted missionary to Calcutta. When he first went to India, the people told him, "How can we listen to the gospel when our stomachs are empty?" More than once we have had children faint in Sunday school because they had not eaten for a few days.

It doesn't work

You'd think that after living for years in Bushwick I'd get used to it, but I don't. When you spend a month with no heat in the middle of winter, you have to work at staying calm.

Who would turn off the heat? No one. The heating system just doesn't work. The infrastructure of New York City is so old the water pipes are exploding, and the sewers are seeping into basements. Steam pipes and boilers give out. There is not enough money to keep up with repairs.

The next question is, "Why do the people stay?" When you grow up in poverty and figure out a way to survive, a move is out of the question. I've met young people living in Brooklyn who have never even been across the East River to Manhattan. How could you convince them to go to Memphis or Minneapolis?

Most people become a reflection of their environment because that is all they know and see. We try to expand their vision. We try to give them some options for their future.

Constant change

The inner city is in a cycle of constant change. Something goes up; something comes down. A business opens and then disappears. We visit children in a tenement, and the next week a new family is there. A month later they have moved on, too. Where do they go? Perhaps they crowd in with relatives—perhaps to a homeless shelter.

In an attempt to understand what these people experience, a staff member and I lived for three days at Grand Central Station, sleeping in the subway corridors. I also spent one night on the steps of the New York Public Library on Fifth Avenue in fifteen degree weather. Homeless people became our friends.

Every person's story has a common thread. As one indigent told me, "I just couldn't face it anymore. I had to get out of the rat race." If they weren't alcoholics when they came to New York, they got that way fast.

The inner-city dilemma was not dealt with when it surfaced in the 1950s and 1960s, and has spread to population centers across our land. I have become tired of reading the words of sociologists and Christian leaders who write about "another generation being lost to street violence." How many generations will we lose before we wake up?

A FLICKER OF LIGHT

The fallen are human too. The lowliest person deserves our kindness, our courtesy and our handshake. People in our neighborhood have tried to make trouble for our program in the past, but I try to show them compassion and love.

The prophet Isaiah was foretelling the life of Christ when he said, "A bruised reed shall he not break, and smoking flax shall he not quench . . ." (Matthew 12:20 KJV). I have yet to meet the person who does not have within him or her a flicker of light or a glimmer of hope. Everyone has the potential for total transformation. "Come now, and let us reason together, saith the Lord: though your sins be as scarlet, they shall be as white as snow; though they be red like crimson, they shall be as wool" (Isaiah 1:18 KJV).

An old hymn by Fanny Crosby called "Rescue the Perishing" holds these words of hope: "Chords that are broken can vibrate once more." Believing this, I plead for the child nobody likes, the one nobody wants to be around. I plead for the teenage girl who is pregnant and not married. I plead for the young man who has fallen into sin. I plead for the mother who has five children by different fathers. Even if there is just a smoking flax, the Lord is not going to put out the fire.

Anyone can be used by God to minister His love in the inner city; a wide-open mission field is on your front doorstep! Tragically, compared to the number of Sunday schools nationwide, there are relatively few inner-city ministries. The explanation is easy: it is hard, sweaty, dirty work. Week after week our staff battles everything from rats to fatigue, from muggings to finding lice in our hair.

At certain times each year on a beach in Australia, thousands of starfish are washed up on the sand. Usually at night, at high tide, a large wave will bring them in so far that the water won't carry them back out. Then, as the sun shines on the starfish, they slowly dry out and die.

One morning a tourist came out of his hotel for a jog at dawn. Down the beach he noticed a little boy picking up stranded starfish and throwing them into the sea. There were thousands of them up and down the shore. The man ran up to the boy and said, "I know what you're doing, and I think I know why you're doing it. Do you really think that what you are doing is going to make a difference?"

Picking up another starfish the boy replied, "I don't know. But I think it will make a difference to this one." And he threw it into the sea.

Multitudes of children in the inner city wait for someone to make a difference in their lives. Children like Patrick whose father is in jail for first-degree murder; Isabel whose mother is in a mental institution because of addiction to drugs; Kim who has permanent scars from the physical abuse she received at age five; Tamara's brother who is on a life-support system because of a bullet lodged in his spine; and Martha and Owen, a brother and sister, who are wards of the state because their parents abandoned them. We can't afford to throw any of these precious children away. Their situations are not hopeless. Listen to what Vincent, age 12, has to say:

> In the news they've been talking about how likely it is for a black male teenager to get shot and killed—especially in my neighborhood. They say it's even more likely that in a couple of years I'll be carrying a gun.
>
> But what they don't know is the difference God's made in my life. Ever since I was three I've been going to Sunday school, and I've learned about God and His ways. And I made up my mind to follow Jesus.

153

No, you'll never see me with a gun shooting anyone. Ever! Because no matter what's going on
around me, I am standing for Jesus!

In a land that has been abundantly blessed, children
everywhere are waiting for a sign that somebody cares. A hurting child is looking for one thing—someone with compassion
and concern, for love shared heart to heart. Do we really care
about them? Or have we turned away, believing we cannot make
a difference?

Every child in America and the world's cities is a perfect patch waiting to become part of the quilt God is making.
We can't afford to throw away a single one.

14

Children and Missions: A Powerful Combination

Peter J. Hohmann with introduction by Jan Bell

Introduction: God uses children

A gang member was walking to the city to meet his gang when suddenly two muggers jumped him, took his money, beat him and ran off.

A nun passed by but totally avoided him. A wealthy man came along, too, but he was far too busy and unconcerned to be bothered, so he walked away.

What would you do? Would you think that your own life might be in peril if you stopped to help? What if the muggers came back? Maybe you would think the gang member got what he deserved, especially if he had hurt others in the past. Would you rush off, pretending you didn't notice the wounded gang member?

If the story sounds familiar, it is the parable of the Good Samaritan retold by orphaned children in Guatemala. When asked to dramatize this story as if it took place in their culture today, they presented this version.

Are you asking yourself, "Well, who's the Good Samaritan?" (We wondered, too.) Who, in their culture, would these children think of as despised and rejected? We were not prepared for their response.

Then a poor child with her donkey came along, saw the poor hurt gang member, and her heart went out to him. She comforted him, bandaged his wounds and helped him onto her donkey. She took him to the local hotel and gave the manager the little money she had to take care of the wounded youth."

The powerful message delivered by this simple little drama struck us all. Here was a poor child offering to do what she could. She knew the pain of the wounded gang member because she had lost count of the number of times she herself had been beaten. She also knew the feelings that come with abandonment and she knew she could not just walk by.

These orphaned children were telling us that each of them is that child. Abandoned? Yes. That's why they are in this place. Rejected? Yes. Each month when family members could visit, the vast majority never do. Beaten? Yes. The children still bear physical as well as emotional scars.

This message that "God wants to use children, especially hurting children, to make a difference in the world today" was the most empowering for these children. Because it came from the children themselves, they could believe it. As adults all we did was create the learning environment for God to speak to the children through his Word.

Even though the words "kids can make a difference" have been more than a catchy phrase for me these past six years, it took a trip to Costa Rica and Guatemala to help me comprehend the magnitude of this message.

The message is *timely.* Everywhere I go I hear people echoing the words "kids ministering to kids." The message is *relevant.* In most countries half the population is 15 years and younger. The message is *needed.* More than 100 million street children roam the world's cities, and countless others are at risk in their own homes.

In the early part of this century God chose bright, energetic, college-educated young people to form the Student Volunteer Movement. They were propelled by a vision to reach into the vast frontiers, forsaking promising careers, wealth and families. Thousands responded by going themselves or sending others. This movement defined missions for most of the 20th century, Now as we approach the year 2000 the question is, "Who will take their place?"

The answer could be children. I believe God wants the next major missions movement to be propelled by children. It is not unusual for God to use the least, the most unassuming and the powerless to extend his kingdom. He's done that countless times throughout history.

My fear is that we may miss the opportunity and our children will be left out of the world-wide missions movement. Is that possible? Yes, it is. When people were looking for a Messiah they expected a king arrayed in power and missed seeing the Christ-child born to a poor family.

We at KIDSCAN believe God has been preparing us for just such a time. We are poised to respond as he leads. Please have your children ready.

CHILDREN AND MISSIONS: A POWERFUL COMBINATION

Children are growing up in a world very different from the one most of us knew. In much of society, acceptance of the absolute truth of the Bible has given way to belief that truth is relative. Life's highest purpose has become self-gratification.

Satan knows if he can rob children of a sense of true purpose he can destroy a generation. We can give children no greater purpose than God's mandate to all believers—to make his name known in all the world.

God promised to make Abraham's lineage a blessing to every people group in the world (Genesis 12:1-3). In Revelation 5 and 7, people from every tribe, tongue and nation are represented before the throne. Between these two passages of Scripture is the story of how God's mandate is accomplished. Children today can have a part in its fulfillment.

157

At a children's missions expo last June, Jan Bell, founder of Kids Can Make A Difference, stated that church workers often view children as the object of *their* ministry, rather than equipping them to *do* the work of ministry. Much of the message given to children helps them feel good about themselves: "God loves me and cares for me; Jesus will help me in times of trouble." These truths are important, but God's purpose for humanity does not stop there.

Bell warns that this me-centered concept can give children the perception of a "tribal god" who works for them alone and who has power limited to their circumstances. Such a narrow view of God leaves little motivation to reach out to others.

Our God, however, is a powerful God; Jesus has been given authority over every tribe, tongue and nation. Furthermore, we are commanded to share him with others (Matthew 28:19). As adults, imparting this purpose to our children is our responsibility and our mission.

The biblical basis of missions is the best place to start training children. God's covenant with Abraham (Genesis 12:1-3) had a top line of blessing and a bottom line of responsibility. God desired to bless Abraham and his descendants, but he also wanted Abraham and his descendants to be a blessing to every nation.

We usually teach children the top-line blessings of the Bible stories, but we fail to teach God's desire to make his name known to every people and nation on earth. For example, often we tell the story of God delivering Daniel in the lion's den, an undeniable story of blessing. Usually, however, the story is left unfinished. The other half of the Abrahamic covenant, Nebuchadnezzar's declaration that all the nations of the world were to worship the God of Daniel, is not told. Every story in the Bible has a top line of blessing and a bottom line of responsibility. We need to teach children both elements.

GIVING CHILDREN A CHRISTIAN WORLD VIEW

One of the greatest challenges in mission education for children is to provide a concrete framework that will enable children to comprehend the abstract nature of world evangelization. The mission "P" words from Kids Can Make A Difference probably do this better than any other device. The goal of the "P" words is to create a missions world view in children. Ten words, each beginning with the letter "P," enable children to understand missions and how to integrate God's purpose into everything around them.

To illustrate, after teaching a lesson from the Sunday school curriculum, or showing a video, the teacher asks the students, "What mission 'P' words did you catch today?" They typically will start shouting, "God's purpose, his power, partnership, people" or other "P" words. Through these "P" words, God's mission of making his name known becomes the lens through which children see the world around them.

To enlarge their world view, children also need to learn about people groups and their religions. Jill Harris, children's director for Destination 2000, uses the acronym THUMB to teach the major blocks of people in the world: "T" is tribals; "H" is Hindus; "U" turned sideways is Chinese; "M" is Muslims and "B" is Buddhists. Display boards with pictures and information can be featured for each group.

Ideally, children can interact directly with people from these groups. A Hindu family shared their life and religion in India with our Sunday school children. They wore traditional clothing and prepared samples of Indian food. The children were fascinated when the Hindu mother showed them her wedding dress and explained that she would not wear it again until her cremation.

Children should always be debriefed after such an interaction to be sure they understand what true Christians believe. Nevertheless, I feel this method is the best way for them to gain a new understanding and compassion for Hindus. Perhaps some will reach out to the Hindu community as a result of their experience.

READING FACILITATES A MISSIONS VISION

The material we read greatly influences our world view. Our church has a missions library. I was surprised to learn that eight out of ten books were checked out by children. Those who are making the greatest impact in missions today are the ones who read the most about missions.

Many new children's books are available to nurture a missions world view. The fourteen-volume *Trailblazer* series, for example, features a fictional child interacting with a real-life missionary. Children need heroes and role models. Why shouldn't they be missionaries, who are some of the greatest of heroes.

HANDS-ON INVOLVEMENT

We have an obligation, a holy responsibility, to educate our children to fulfill God's purpose. As Christian leaders, our responsibility is to promote the attitude that direct involvement in God's purposes is the norm.

Passing on theoretical knowledge alone, however, is not enough. Children need direct, hands-on involvement in missions. The consequences of not directly involving children in outreach and missions is reflected in the lives of many adults. Children's programs have often emphasized three things: sitting still, being quiet and listening.

Should we be surprised when, as adults, they continue to do what they have been taught? By the time children reach adulthood, almost all their attitudes are formed. Why not form in the child the attitude that direct involvement in God's purpose is the norm?

The children who are most excited about their faith are those who are provided hands-on opportunities for involvement in God's purpose. Without active involvement in sharing the gospel, children often become bored with Christianity. Through direct involvement, the truths a child hears in the classroom are tested in real-life circumstances and become proven knowledge.

God wants to use children today, but in reality much of our emphasis with children is future-oriented. Success is often measured only by what a child does after he or she is an adult, but God wants to use children today to make a difference in the world.

A 12-year-old girl in our church proved God's desire and ability to use children. At age nine, she was burdened for Mongolia while doing a school assignment on that country. She was moved that a whole nation existed with only a handful of believers.

After two years of faithful intercession, she saw a mission magazine at church with the words "Hope for Mongolia" written in bold letters across the cover. The article described a crusade in Mongolia where 500 people were saved. She was excited! She knew that those words, "Hope for Mongolia," were God's way of telling her he had heard her prayer; her name is Hope Smith.

Revival had indeed started in Mongolia and the 500 believers have grown into a flourishing church of over 1,000 people. The church's name? Hope Assembly. God does answer the prayers of a child!

The question arises, "Should children be allowed to go on mission trips?" Six years ago we began including children, accompanied by their parents, in mission trips. Some of the children joining us on international trips have been as young as eight years old. They helped with children's ministry in the inner city or with Vacation Bible Schools in several Latin American countries. Their experiences were positive and several of these children now desire to be career missionaries.

BRIDGE BUILDERS

Yes, I am convinced that children need to be integrated into mission teams. But what about a mission team composed entirely of children? Our church became convinced that God wanted us to involve our children in this way. After examining different models for this type of ministry, we chose the one used by King's Kids International, affiliated with Youth With A Mission.

The goal of King's Kids is the discipleship of children in the context of outreach and missions. We didn't want to just "use" children for outreach, we wanted to disciple them to hear God's leading and to obey him. Furthermore, we wanted the children's outreach to be a natural outgrowth of their worship. As if that wasn't enough, we also wanted a team where entire families could minister together. King's Kids provided the training to achieve all these goals, and Bridge Builders, a King's Kids Go Network team composed of children ages 6-18 years, was born!

Bridge Builders main method of ministry in the inner city is worshiping God with contemporary songs set to choreography. They also minister through the performing arts, intercession and practical service. We believe that people are drawn to God as they see true worship, especially from children. A typical program might consist of an hour of songs and testimonies followed by the children praying individually with people.

This approach may sound like one that would work only in a church-service setting, but I have witnessed these children praying for people and leading them to Christ even in shopping malls.

The team conducts a major two-week outreach each summer plus bimonthly outreaches throughout the year. An outreach always consists of being together all weekend to provide time for discipleship, worship, rehearsal and preparation of the children's hearts for ministry.

Bridge Builders has ministered in housing projects, nursing homes, shopping malls, hospices for the dying, rehabilitation centers, homeless shelters, city parks and even at the beach. Sometimes ministry consists of cleaning an elderly woman's yard in the inner city or playing basketball with kids in a housing project.

I have observed children making a difference. And the children who participate in these mission outreaches are different! Their Sunday school teachers have commented on how they are the first in class to pray or share what God is doing in their lives. They have a greater sensitivity to God and to those around them than they had before. They often speak about impressions and thoughts that God gives them and are eager to share Bible verses that speak to their hearts.

In a world where children are often self-centered, the Bridge Builders program has developed within children a compassion for others. I have watched them hold hands with the homeless, praying simple prayers for their protection and provision.

When we conducted outreaches in shopping malls, I felt in my heart that nothing important would happen. But later, in debriefing, the children shared incredible testimonies of praying for people's needs and even leading some to Christ. They pray easily with others, even those they have just met.

On a recent nursing home outreach, my 14-year-old daughter shared her experience with a feeble, elderly woman. "I looked at her," my daughter said, "and I saw a little girl. I realized she was really no different from me." The children are taking a second look at the people around them and are aware of their need for Jesus.

Sometimes our children have wrong attitudes. During these times I am tempted to question the validity of the deep changes I am privileged to witness in their lives. I was thinking about this during a recent outreach.

As the children arrived at our church with sleeping bags tucked under their arms, they were running around acting like typical hyperactive kids. At that moment, they seemed so unspiritual! To top it all, the previous outreach hadn't gone well. After worship and prayer, however, some of the children gave testimonies of what God had done in their lives the previous week. As they shared, all doubt in my heart disappeared.

One teenage girl shared how she had led a friend to Christ; an 11-year-old had witnessed to several of his friends on the school bus; and, most incredible, another teenage girl had petitioned the school board to start a Bible club. She was granted permission, and later the first meeting was held with 25 students attending!

Other children shared how God was speaking to them individually and as a group, through various Scriptures. Children of all ages led out in prayer and initiated worship songs. Anyone who works with children knows that such acts of prayer, praise and witness don't occur naturally.

A ministry like Bridge Builders will be hard and, at times, discouraging. But when children are discipled in the context of missions, real change does occur in their lives.

I firmly believe that children are on the cutting edge of world evangelism in our church and are having an impact on the church as a whole. Before we began our Bridge Builders team, it was difficult to involve adults in inner-city outreach. When the children began to minister in the inner city, the parents were quick to follow.

Baby Boomer parents will commit themselves to activities that interest their children. Look at the way parents shuttle their children to every after-school activity and sports practice. Why not to mission activities? Since the King's Kids model is based on the family structure, and entire families are encouraged to be involved, it is especially effective in involving adults in missions. Other ministries in our church also are beginning to follow the pattern of discipling young people in the context of missions.

Ownership is the key to success in ministry. Adults who work with a group such as Bridge Builders are like cheerleaders on the sidelines. The children have learned to take ownership of the ministry by hearing from God and learning to obey him. Not uncommonly a child will share with the group what he or she feels God is leading the group to do. Children take personal responsibility for their lives, and for fulfilling God's purposes.

This process has been radically different from the entertainment model which many children's programs employ. On occasion, when things weren't going well, the adult leaders even left the room, telling the youth to work things out between themselves and God. This might sound like an invitation to chaos, but often in these times God moves mightily through the children.

An ongoing performing-arts team composed of children is a big undertaking. A year of program building preceded our first two-week outreach. I am convinced that the price paid in time and resources is worthwhile. Nevertheless, it may be wise to start with something more manageable than an ongoing team.

PRAYING AND PRAYER WALKS

You could organize a prayer walk through your town or city, or conduct a prayer walk without ever leaving the building! Kids enjoy praying in challenging places, such as where battles or historical events occurred. During times of prayer, God often impresses them with what is happening in the heavenlies.

During a recent Concert of Prayer, we decided to invite the children of our city. The emphasis focused on praying for the 100 gateway cities of the 10/40 window. Each "city" was a room decorated with artifacts, pictures and prayer points for the particular city.

The children visited and prayed for eight cities; they also tasted the food or heard music from these cities. Most importantly, they were able to identify enough with each city to pray effectively.

Children can also pray for people groups and nations. Guides, such as Jill Johnstone's *You Can Change the World*, are helpful in providing information. This book lists seven prayer points for each people group or country. Reading the accompanying prayers can be an easy way for children to learn to pray for people groups or nations.

MOBILIZERS AND MISSION SENDERS

Children can also be mission "mobilizers" in mission conventions and other special events. Children and youth can perform dramas and sing in choirs for mission conventions or make mission presentations in their Sunday school classes. Bridge Builders mobilizes other churches by conducting Go Camps. During a Go Camp, children from another church participate in a weekend outreach. This contact can be the first step in pioneering more teams like Bridge Builders.

Children also can be mission "senders" participating in mission fund raisers and in weekly or monthly mission giving. The children in our denomination gave over two million dollars to missions last year through a special program called "Boys and Girls Missionary Crusade." That's a lot of small change!

EQUIPPING CHILDREN FOR SERVICE

The way the church views children's ministry is due for a paradigm shift. The church needs to equip children to fulfill God's purposes. The way God accomplishes his purpose has always held an element of surprise. Could it be that he desires to use children to usher in a mighty move of his Spirit across the world? I am convinced that a special anointing rests on this generation of youth. Perhaps it is their simple faith and innocent hearts, or maybe God has chosen the weak and foolish things to shame the wise.

Either way, I believe the children living today will be the ones to bring closure to the Great Commission. They are not only a generation of destiny but also a generation that God is using this very moment. As adults, we have been called to equip them to fulfill God's purpose: to know him and make him known; to redeem a people from every people; to establish a Kingdom over every kingdom.

As one girl testified at the end of a summer outreach, "I knew that kids could make a difference, but I didn't think they could make a big difference. Now I know we can make a big difference."

15

The Littlest Prayer Warriors

Esther Ilnisky and Karen Moran

A new breed of children, a righteous seed, is emerging all over the world, who are sovereignly destined to fulfill God's end-time purposes for them. Entrusted to godly parents and spiritual mentors for nurturing, training and equipping, they are rising as a mighty prayer force to petition God for their generation. We are witnesses to this marvel everywhere we go. We hear of it happening all over the world.

Recognizing and nurturing a child's spirituality has the potential of releasing the church's most untapped resource of prayer power. "Make room for the children," Jesus declared. "Do not hinder them! Let them come to me" (Mark 10:14). Simply stated, "Let them pray." Is that not the way we "come to him" today? Children really love to pray! Please let them!

A currently familiar phrase is "Save the children!" Jesus affirmed the children when they shouted "Hosanna, Hosanna" (Matthew 21:15-16). The root meaning of "hosanna" is "God save us!" We hear the children shouting it again today, fulfilling the words Jesus quoted: "From the lips of children and infants you have ordained praise . . . to silence the foe and the avenger" (Psalm 8:2).

Nearly two billion children ages 12 and under will be alive on Planet Earth by the year 2000. Our goal is to have millions of godly children join forces with our Children's Global Prayer Movement to "CATCH THE VISION—GET GLOBAL!" The call is for children to become world-shapers, to pray for their generation and to silence THEIR foes and avengers. As Isaiah says, "a little child will lead them" (Isaiah 11:6).

What are some practical ways to teach children about prayer? Begin by teaching them the important place prayer has in causing their personal healing. James 5:16 voices the biblical principle that when we pray for one another, we, too, will be healed.

Encourage children with the fact that they understand better and can pray more effectively for other children because they experience similar things firsthand. (Often children think that, because of their age, adults can pray better.)

Praying for other children will lift them outside themselves. Instead of petitioning only for their own needs, their problems and their concerns, they can focus on others. Teach children that as they temporarily forget their own needs to pray for others, Jesus will meet their needs, too. Children need to know that it is not important for them to pray with many words, but it is important that they pray the words from their hearts.

To prepare their hearts for prayer, ask children to place their hands over their hearts and speak to the Lord. "Here is my heart, Lord. If it is not clean, I ask that you cleanse it." Ask them to do the same with their hands according to Psalm 24:3-4. This action signifies right attitudes and motives.

Explain that they do not have to be concerned about having lots of experience in praying. Remind them of the little boy in the Bible story in John 6. All this boy had to give Jesus was five barley loaves and two fish. Look what happened, though! Jesus took what the little boy gave and multiplied it. The results? Jesus fed five thousand men plus the women and children and had twelve baskets of bread left over. God takes what we give him and multiplies it.

Instruct children in the habit of praying specific, targeted prayers. They can—

- ask the Father in Jesus' name to heal the physical needs of children: addiction to drugs, alcohol, hunger, poverty, disease and entanglement in the sex industry.

- ask the Father in Jesus' name to heal the emotional needs of children: healing from physical and verbal abuse, rejection and abandonment.

- ask the Father to reveal how much he loves and unconditionally accepts children.

- ask the Father in Jesus' name to draw other children unto salvation.

- pray for missionaries and evangelists to be sent into the harvest. Stress that missions is a priority on God's heart. He could even use *them* to be missionaries and evangelists.

- pray that Christian children will tell others about Jesus.

- pray that God would supernaturally reveal himself to children and adults in Muslim and other nations where missionaries are scarce. (We have heard reports of Jesus appearing to Muslim children and even healing them of diseases. As a result, whole families have turned to Christ.)

- pray about things going on in the world. Use magazines, newspapers, TV news, maps of your city, state or even the world. Use as many visuals as possible.

(Esther Network International has many prayer tools to help you. See Appendix A for more information.)

- pray over the TV, videos, magazines, books, toys and such that influence children in an evil way.

- pray for leaders, including local, state, national and world.

- pray about issues such as unity in families, churches, among different Christian denominations, races and ethnic groups.

- pray for those in the 10/40 window, the area between 10 and 40 degrees north latitude across the top of Africa, the Middle East and Asia. In this area of the world—

  — more than 90 percent of unreached people live,

  — the poorest of the poor struggle to survive, and

  — three major religious strongholds exist, Buddhism, Hinduism and Islam.

- pray whatever the Holy Spirit puts upon your heart (Romans 8:26-27).

Remember to keep specific goals and prayer events in mind. We participated in a "Night of Power" to pray for the Muslim world. These seasons of prayer can last from an hour to all night, and their frequency can be flexible. An awesome anointing often comes upon the children as God places the burden of his heart upon them during these times.

Use songs as prayers and worship to "silence the foe and the avenger" (Psalm 8:2). Songs with this focus could include *No Other Name, Jesus Loves the Little Children* or *Shine, Jesus, Shine.*

Other strategies to help children in prayer include:

- five-year-olds praying for other five-year-olds.

- praying for other children who have your first name. (Remember to use foreign names with equivalent English meanings. For example, Miguel or Michel for Michael.)

- street children praying for other street children.

- children who are victims of violence or abuse praying for other such children. Prayer can include their protection and deliverance from harmful environments.

Encourage children to stay global in their prayers. Covering in their prayers all the children in the world with similar problems is as easy as just praying for themselves. Their prayers could include: "Lord, I pray for John and me. We are having a problem with fear, but I also pray for all the other boys and girls in the world who are having this problem. Set us all free. Thank you, Lord, for hearing my prayer."

Help the children recognize areas that need prayer by asking questions. What are some world problems or concerns? Identify problems or concerns that children their ages are going through. What are some things to pray for one another? Some children at first may not want to admit they personally are having a problem. Don't force them to respond if it is too uncomfortable for them. Many will open up and share their concerns in private when they know they can trust you.

The ultimate goal is for children to achieve a confidence in prayer. Then they can have their own prayer times anytime or anywhere. Let them learn to hear from the Lord about what is on his heart, discovering that which they should include in their prayers.

The following statements are helpful for imparting confidence in prayer to the hearts and minds of children.

To children everywhere:

- Do you know that praying children can be "world shapers"? (That's our special name for you!)

- Do you know that Jesus says the kingdom of God belongs to you? He has a very special love for you. When he lived on earth, he always blessed the children. Jesus held children on his lap and talked to them. He listened to children. Jesus even put them in front of people and drew attention to them. You can pray to Jesus! He'll listen to you!

- Jesus wants you to be a house of prayer. Jesus lives in you and you are his "house." You can be what the prophet Isaiah said: "My house shall be called a house of prayer for all peoples" (Isaiah 56:7 RSV).

- When children pray, things begin to happen. God said, "Ask for the nations and I will give them to you" (Psalm 2:8). Jesus needs YOU to be one of the millions joining the children's global prayer movement—a great army, one awesome house of prayer for the world. He wants you to love all the children of the world and pray for their salvation.

The following are examples of children who have had specific things shown to them while in earnest prayer before the Lord:

Lindsay, while lying prostrate before the Lord, saw Tibetan children. She said the Lord told her they were helpless and homeless.

Kelly, ten, while holding a Globall (a soft huggable globe of the world), began to weep. The Lord had shown her child victims of war who had lost arms and legs.

Bennie, eight, prays regularly over the 10/40 Window regions of the world. Once he saw angels go to Hindu children, who were worshiping idols, to tell them about Jesus.

Jesse, seven, while in prayer witnessed violent people stopped by God from killing.

Mary, while praying, saw Muslim children. The Lord said to her, "I have four words for you: THEY DON'T KNOW ME." She began to pray for their salvation.

In the Philippines, forty young prayer warriors, 7-12 years old, groaned and travailed for the lost, the victims of injustices, the poor and the street children.

The praying children of the Global Consultation on World Evangelism (GCOWE '95) in Seoul, Korea were an historic first for a conference of this magnitude. Forty-three of GCOWE's most serious and distinctive official delegates from eight nations were 15 years old or younger.

Dazzling flashbacks continue to appear before me. I see and hear the children, prostrate before the Lord in intense weeping and spiritual warfare for the lost for extended periods of time—sometimes up to four hours. I see the responses from adult world leaders as the children laid hands on them and prayed for them with supernatural wisdom.

Visibly moved, many said they had never had a child pray for them before. I see the resplendent look on Dr. Peter Wagner's face as anointed, praying children literally converged on him. Like an echo, I hear them shouting, "Yes!" to put a seal of agreement on every prayer.

The children knew no cultural, social, age or spiritual barriers. I learned a valuable lesson from them: even language barriers didn't hinder these prayer warriors. These remarkable children came to pray together . . . and that they did! Uppermost in my mind is the memory of the before-and-after stories as one by one they expressed how their lives had been touched and changed because of this time together. One boy stated, "My blessing from Korea is getting stronger." Another said, "When the members of the International Children's Prayer Track drop to their knees, God shows up, bringing healing and hope."

In his sovereign genius, God brought together for this major event exactly the praying children he had chosen. From the foundations of the earth he planned for them to make this prophetic statement to, I believe, the entire Christian world: "I am raising up the children to be a new generation of intercessors and prayer warriors for the end-time revival and harvest. Make room for them!"

God is truly raising a standard against the myriad onslaughts arrayed against this generation. I challenge you to teach the children, then let them lead their generation out of the darkness that surrounds them through powerful, God-directed prayer. Only eternity will tell the story of the multitudes of lives touched by the prayers of children.

Part 4

Equipping for Ministry

16

Counseling the Wounded Child

Edward T. Welch

*Y*ou are the counselor for wounded children. In a world of professionals and specialists we often refer such children to experts, but God's Word indicates that those who have his Spirit and know his Word are the experts. You have both the ability and the responsibility to counsel wounded children.

This does not mean that you will schedule one-hour-a-week office appointments with children. Biblical counseling is much broader than the counseling typically practiced in places like the United States. It can last a few minutes, or it can consist of many hours over a period of years. Time and place are unimportant. Biblical counseling is the private ministry of God's Word. Its goal is to understand the unique situation of a child's life and, with love and compassion, match life themes with relevant biblical teaching.

Perhaps some people avoid counseling wounded children because they feel poorly equipped to help, especially when confronted with children who have experienced a life of tragedy and pain. Yet the plain truths of Scripture are sufficient for in-depth counsel. The following will review these basic biblical truths for counseling wounded children by asking three questions:

1. Who is the child?
2. What does the child need?
3. What are some methods for counseling children?

WHO IS THE CHILD?

Biblical counsel begins by answering the question, Who is the child? From a biblical perspective, the answer is relatively simple. Children are best understood from two perspectives: sinned against and sinner. To be more precise, children are both shaped by innumerable external influences (such as the sins of others), and they have hearts that worship either God or idols. Both perspectives are essential to biblical counseling. If counselors examine only shaping influences, children will be hopeless victims, powerless before the onslaught of further oppression. At most, counseling would offer social support and compassion; it could not go deeply to the heart. On the other hand, if counselors consider only the spiritual allegiances of children's hearts, children will not benefit from the rich Scripture that gives practical guidance and comfort in the midst of victimization.

This book pays special attention to some of the more destructive shaping influences such as parental abandonment, neglect by the state, poverty, physical abuse and sexual abuse. These are certainly hazardous shaping influences, but they are not exhaustive. For example, riches can be as influential and detrimental as poverty. In the Scripture riches are often the greater curse. What about influences imposed by the physical body? More noticeable ones include paralysis, disfigurement from injury and malnutrition. Less noticeable physical influences include differences in intellectual and learning abilities. For example, some children cannot memorize well or do not remember a biblical principle that you taught them an hour ago. Some children might remember things they see much better than things they hear. Other children learn best by doing.

Counselors can never have an exhaustive understanding of the influences in a child's life. Shaping influences—for good and bad—from just one month of age could fill volumes. As such, counselors do not examine every detail of a child's life. Instead, they are interested students of the child, piecing together the most salient and memorable influences so that these forces can be addressed by God's Word.

The second perspective on the child comes from the study of Scripture more than by the study of the child. It is the view from the heart. This is not the physical heart. Rather, it is the spiritual center, the wellspring of life (Proverbs 4:23). It is the place where we stand at a crossroads between the worship of God and the worship of our own desires or idols. The heart is righteous or sinful, receptive to truth or hard, full of faith or full of unbelief. At the level of the heart, children are no differ-ent from adults. They are constantly confronted with the ques-tion, "Who will you worship?"

This idea is biblical, but it raises another question: How can we expect children to understand such sophisticated theo-logical concepts? Most adults don't think in these terms, let alone children. Spiritual understanding, however, is not de-pendent on an ability to think abstractly. It does not take great intellectual ability to know that we are worshipers. For ex-ample, James 4:1-10 is a classic discussion about the human heart. It asks, "What causes fights and quarrels among you?" To this we could add, "What causes temper tantrums, jeal-ousy, cruel anger and selfishness?" The answer: "You want some-thing but you don't get it." You are worshiping your desires rather than submitting to God. Not only do children understand that they can have a bad case of the "I wantsies," they often under-stand it better than adults. Adults have a long history of practice with rationalization and blame-shifting. If we are in a quarrel, it's the *other* person's fault, and we will defend our excuses to ex-tremes. Children are not so experienced in their sin, and their instinctive sense of right and wrong—their conscience—is often precise in its judgments of their own sin. Children are usually quick to see their pervasive "I wantsies."

When counseling children, one task is to flesh out these two categories. You should have a ready answer to both questions: What are the unique influences that have shaped this person? and, What selfish desires tend to ensnare the child? When you understand shaping influences, the child will feel understood. When you understand the bent of the heart, you will be able to point the child to Jesus and give hope.

WHAT DOES THE CHILD NEED?

Given these two perspectives on children, it follows that they have a handful of basic needs. One essential need for children who have been victimized is *they must know what God says about their victimization.* Children may be astute in discerning their own sin, but they are usually very shallow in their ability to sort out responsibility when they have been sinned against. Too often, they follow the logic of Job's comforters: bad things happen to bad people. "Bad things happened to me, therefore I am a bad person." They think that they are getting what they deserve. When they understand that they have been sinned against by a person, they are quick to believe, especially if the prominent victimizer is someone close to them, that they caused the other person's sin. "If I'd been silent, Daddy wouldn't have beat me," or "The reason Mr. ____ is making me do this is because I've been bad." Wounded children must understand that they are not capable of causing other people to sin against them. Instead, the sins of others are caused by their own hearts, not by the children's.

Not only does God tell children they are not the cause of the oppressor's sin, God also tells children that he is against the oppressor and he is for the oppressed. He is for those who have no advocates, such as children, widows and the poor. He is the Good Shepherd who brings woe to the shepherds who destroyed and scattered the sheep (Jeremiah 23:1-4), and he promises to tend his flock with justice. "I will rescue my flock"; "I myself will search for my sheep"; "I will pasture them"; "I will bind up the injured and strengthen the weak." These are God's promises to his wounded children (Ezekiel 34:1-16).

182

With responsibility clarified, *children need to know what God says to sinners like themselves.* Does this seem like an added weight to children who are already hurting? Theologically, most people would say "no"; but practically, counselors are reluctant to talk about sin with people who have been victimized. Granted, it is not necessarily the first item on a biblical agenda, but to ignore the guilt of sin is to further victimize children.

Children typically have surprising insight into their own sin, and they are often more willing than adults to talk about it. Their consciences have made it clear to them that they have violated God's law. They need to confess that sin is against God and, most importantly, to know the gospel. They must know the biblical teaching that is "of first importance: that Christ died for our sins according to the Scriptures, that he was buried, that he was raised on the third day according to the Scriptures, and that he appeared to Peter, and then to the Twelve" (1 Corinthians 15:3-5). If there is only one thing you communicate in your counseling, this is it. You want to teach children that the answer to every question is "Jesus." You want them to know that, through the gospel, God adopts those who believe so that he is no longer just *God*, but he is *my God*. He belongs to me and I belong to him. He is *my Father* and I am his child (1 John 3:1).

For the wounded child suffering does not disappear, but it is outweighed by the increasingly glorious knowledge of Christ and our eternal hope (2 Corinthians 4:17). Counselors must have more expertise in talking about Jesus than in techniques to deal with suffering and pain.

A third need is for children to listen to Jesus and do what he says. They must learn to obey. Even better, *children need to learn to love God's law.* God's law is not the gospel, but it is an expression of God's righteous character. Therefore, it is something beautiful and to be reverenced. To make it even more beautiful, the law teaches us how to love God. It is as if God says, "Now that you have seen what I have done for you,

you will want to love me in return. You can do that by obeying my law."

Obedience is not done out of a fear of punishment, because there must never be fear of punishment in those who know the love of Jesus (1 John 4:18). Obedience comes out of a grateful heart that responds to God's loving initiative. It proceeds from reverential fear and respect. It proceeds from our worship of God.

A common mistake is for counselors to forget the attractiveness of the law. In this generation many people are more concerned about legalism than licentiousness. They contrast the law with the freedom we have in Christ, and they point to the apostle Paul's absolute loathing of the law. We must remember, however, that what Paul hated was the idea that we could find righteousness by obeying the law. Such works-righteousness was against the essence of the gospel of grace. Paul, like King David, loved God's law when used rightly (cf. Psalm 119). He knew that God's law blesses us by teaching us how to be imitators of his righteousness and how to see our own sin so we can be brought to our need for Jesus.

God's greatest gift is Jesus. As if that isn't enough, he gives us his law. Children should be taught that they are part of the royal family, and the King is blessing them with a great gift—a gift that teaches them how to love God and love others. They can honor the King by loving that gift.

These three basic needs hover around the three poles of knowledge of self, knowledge of God and knowledge of others. Of these three, the knowledge of God is the greatest. Self-knowledge and the knowledge of others follow from our knowledge of God. Wasn't the greatest responsibility of Hebrew parents to teach their children about the mighty acts of God? They had yearly Passovers and many other feast days which were intended to review these great acts. They had weekly Sabbaths that pointed to God's creative and sustaining power. Parents were commanded to have the great works of God always on their lips.

Wasn't it the lack of this knowledge that led to the Israelite catastrophes? Generation after generation forsook their responsibility to pass on the knowledge of God. Notice, for example, how this happened almost immediately. As soon as Joshua and his generation died, "another generation grew up, who knew neither the Lord nor what he had done for Israel" (Judges 2:10). This is truly one of the great tragedies in the Scripture, and it stands as an example of our own tendency to desert those things that are of first importance. Our goal is for children to *own* the true God and the gospel. We want children to be like the friends of the Samaritan woman who said, "We no longer believe just because of what you said; now we have heard for ourselves, and we know that this man really is the Savior of the world" (John 4:42).

SOME METHODS FOR COUNSELING CHILDREN

These basic biblical truths establish the substance or content of all biblical counseling, but this content must be delivered with biblical methods or it will be dry and wooden. The method, of course, can be summarized as *love*.

The Bible commands us to love all people, so a specific call to love children and the oppressed is unnecessary. But God *does* underline the command to love and protect children. Most likely the Bible emphasizes this because we are prone to favoritism and partiality. In our ministries we tend to be attracted to people who are more like us, who are attractive or who are influential and powerful. While children may be physically attractive, they are certainly neither like us nor influential and powerful.

The disciples evidenced such partiality. The ministry of Jesus, they assumed, was adult-driven. Its intent was to bring the kingdom to Israel, and that meant influencing the masses and winning over some of the leaders. When people began to bring children to Jesus, the disciples' mission statement did not include such ministry. Ministry to children had no pay-off. But characteristic of his entire ministry, Jesus did the unexpected. He welcomed children and elevated them (Mark 9:37, 10:16). He did much more than remind the disciples that children, too, need the bread of life. He gave them a vivid picture of blessing the children, and he told the disciples that they must become like children.

Therefore, the method for counseling children is to love them in the name of Jesus. Loving them means welcoming and blessing them. The Bible further suggests that it means enjoying them. The example of Jesus is that he embraced them. They were not a drain on his ministry; they were a delight. Furthermore, ministry to children is not like ministry to skeptical adults. Children display a praiseworthy openness and spiritual insight. They demonstrate the naturalness of the knowledge of God (Romans 1:19-21). They often understand spiritual stories that mystify adults. Professional counselors would be willing to pay for such counselees.

Within this circle of love and enjoyment are a handful of specific methods that counselors should consider: counseling should be concrete, creative and celebratory.

Concrete counseling

Concrete means teaching directed toward the senses. You want children to see, feel, hear, taste or touch the truth. For example, let's say that you want to encourage a shy child to be an ambassador for Jesus. You could say, "Johnny, let's start thinking about your family more. This week you can work on loving them." Jesus makes this teaching concrete when he says, "You, Johnny, are the light of the world." We talk about abstract concepts such as love; Jesus talks about the Good Samaritan. We talk about a sovereign God; Jesus directs our attention to the birds, lilies and grass as evidence of his sovereign care.

Churches are edified by children's sermons because they are concrete. Jesus is praised by unbelieving educators because his teaching is concrete. When instructing or comforting a child in the knowledge of God, make sure it touches the senses. The more senses involved the more memorable the story.

186

Creative counseling

Counseling should also be creative. This means that you are continually thinking about new ways to impart well-known material. This concept is especially important when you wisely choose to focus on just a few basic points. Remember, the teachings in Christianity are not new, and the propositions we want children to know are few. We want them to know God as Creator and Redeemer, themselves as sinners who have been adopted by faith and others as neighbors and recipients of our debt of love. To keep these truths fresh and memorable demands creativity.

For example, when talking about love, you can read the story of the Good Samaritan; you can act it out; you can write a song about it; you can pray for each other to love like the Samaritan; and you can tell stories about when other people treated you like the Samaritan treated his enemy. One of the problems in much of modern teaching is that we receive too much information. We hear at least one sermon on Sunday, another on Wednesday, a third on the radio, and each sermon is on a different subject. Creative instruction could meditate on one teaching for weeks, months or even years.

Celebratory counseling

A third essential method for counseling the wounded child is that counseling must ultimately be celebratory. This doesn't mean that we smile at the effects of evil and always remind the child that all things work together for good. It means that Christ has risen; he has paid the penalty we deserved; he has adopted us as his children; and he has given us the Holy Spirit who assures us of our home in the presence of God for eternity. If we lived in a world where each day was the same as the last, we would have no cause for celebration, but we are promised that "in just a very little while" (Hebrews 10:37) Jesus will come and usher in eternity. For the person in pain, it is the pain of childbirth. This pain is, indeed, severe, but it is outweighed by the great blessing almost in view.

Celebration can mean having a party because of what Jesus has done. It can mean lively worship songs. It can mean eating a meal together practicing for the wedding feast of the Lamb. It can mean making colorful posters and decorating a room. The apostle Paul said, "Rejoice in the Lord always" (Philippians 4:4). This statement is a powerful one from a person in prison. No matter where he would have placed such an exhortation in his letter, it would have been a shocking statement. So it is even more remarkable when he immediately follows up this exhortation with, "I will say it again: Rejoice!"

Children tend to be good rejoicers. Even children who have been severely hurt are good rejoicers. In this way they are examples to adults; they remind us of the upcoming heavenly celebration that will last forever. Counselors should nurture this God-given ability.

With these guidelines in mind, the church must be unleashed on the world's children. Children need godly counsel and encouragement. Too often, those who counsel with an adult have realized that the best time for counseling was when the person was a child. When they were children many people started to believe myths about God, themselves and other people. It was then they started to believe that because of their sin their parents abandoned them. They started to believe that they were like Cinderella before God, that is, they lived in the basement and were never really family. Many counselors in the church are praying that God would raise men and women to counsel these children before such myths take root.

You are the counselors. Better yet, you are God's priests. You invite children to know the presence of God. You have the privilege of pronouncing the priestly blessing over them (Numbers 6:22-27). And you can follow Christ by literally laying hands on them and blessing them. There is, however, one significant way in which you will be different from an Old Testament priest. In the Old Testament, the priest blessed and the people received the blessing. Now, you bless, but you are also given a blessing from children who have a remarkable ability to grasp moral and spiritual truths.

188

17

Interventions:
An Holistic Approach

Perry Downs

Interventions for children in difficult circumstances must be holistic and compassionate. Compassion means to enter into the suffering of another person. The word means literally *to suffer with*. Being compassionate means being willing to feel the pain of others, and to bear the pain of others. We bear this pain, not in a redemptive sense of suffering on their behalf (Jesus did that), but rather in the loving sense of entering into their world.

When the Father sent the Son to earth, he was sent to enter into our world as it actually is. He was a "man of sorrows, and familiar with suffering" (Isaiah 53:3). He modeled for us compassion and taught that we should "be merciful, just as your Father is merciful" (Luke 6:36).

Anyone who works with children victimized by situations they cannot control knows the pain of entering into their world. To see the pain (or worse, the emptiness) in the eyes of these little ones causes any sensitive person to hurt with the child. Responses of anger, frustration, hopelessness or despair are common in those who work with abused and traumatized children. We see firsthand the inhumanity of adults to children and must wonder about the evil that lurks in the human heart. And, we sometimes wonder where God is in the midst of the carnage. Does he see, and does he care? A compassionate response causes us to feel and ask these questions.

Interventions must also be holistic, that is, ministering to the whole child. Physical needs, such as food, shelter, clothing and safety, must be addressed. These necessities can be some of the most urgent and time consuming concerns. In addition, children must be reached emotionally, helping them learn to trust, love and become "attached" to others. Socially, the children must learn to live in relation to a larger group, and learn to be contributing members of their society. Morally, children must learn to know right from wrong, and to consider others as they make their moral decisions. But the interventions will not be complete unless the spiritual needs of the child are also met. Children must be taught to respond to God's love and to allow the love of God to bring healing and redemption. Interventions must be holistic.

DEFINING CHRISTIAN NURTURE

The term *Christian nurture* refers to ministry designed to address the spiritual needs of a person. To *nurture* means to care for, nourish, sustain or cultivate. *Christian nurture* means to cultivate and sustain Christian faith in another person.

Because all people are made in the image of God, all persons have great significance. All people, regardless of nationality, race, social context or ability, have dignity and worth. All people matter, because all people bear God's image.

But having worth and dignity is not the same as being God's children. The Bible teaches that human beings are born separated from God because of sin, and that we must be reborn into the family of God. The Bible speaks clearly of two categories of humankind; those who are the children of God, and those who are not.

Jesus said to Nicodemus, "I tell you the truth, unless a man is born again, he cannot see the kingdom of God" (John

3:3). When Nicodemus was confused by this statement, Jesus explained that this second birth must be "of the Spirit." That is, we must be reborn by the Spirit of God to be God's child. Jesus went on to make a startling statement:

> For God so loved the world that he gave his one and only Son, that whoever believes in him shall not perish but have eternal life. For God did not send his Son into the world to condemn the world, but to save the world through him. Whoever believes in him is not condemned, but whoever does not believe stands condemned already because he has not believed in the name of God's one and only Son (John 3:16-18).

Jesus affirmed God's love for humankind, and established that not all people belong to God's family. There are those who stand condemned and those who are no longer condemned. The difference is based on belief in Jesus.

John made this same point earlier in the gospel when he wrote regarding Jesus:

> He was in the world, and though the world was made through him, the world did not recognize him. He came to that which was his own, but his own did not receive him. Yet to all who received him, to those who believed in his name, he gave the right to become children of God—children born not of natural descent, nor of human decision or a husband's will, but born of God (John 1:10-13).

John insisted that not all people belong to God in the same way. All are created by God and valued by God—but only those who believe in Jesus can be called the children of God. We must be born again by the Spirit to be removed from condemnation and to become God's children.

Those who would nurture faith in children must understand that not all children have faith and not all children belong to God in the same sense. Some children will need to be led to Jesus so they might believe and become God's child, and others will need to have developed the faith they already hold. Christian nurture in this sense will include both evangelizing children to bring them to faith and nurturing others to a stronger, more mature faith.

DEFINING THE GOSPEL

Christian ministry is about proclaiming the gospel—the good news of redemption in Jesus. The heart of the gospel is that God's wrath, his holy anger towards sin, has been appeased and that through faith in Christ we can become his children. The Apostle John explained it this way:

> And this is the testimony: God has given us eternal life, and this life is in his Son. He who has the Son has life; he who does not have the Son of God does not have life (1 John 5:11-12).

While it is true that all people stand condemned as sinners before a holy God, it is also true that God offers us forgiveness through Christ. Our primary need is to have our sins forgiven, to be freed from the wrath of God. Jesus' death on the cross provides forgiveness, if we believe. God has provided for our redemption, but we must believe.

THE MEANING OF BELIEF

What does it mean to believe—to have faith in Jesus? How do we receive Christ, moving from condemnation to life and continue to be nurtured in the faith? The Bible talks about belief or faith in three different ways. The three together make up the substance of faith.

First, faith has a content—there is something to be believed. There is truth to be accepted. In other words, we must believe the right things to be saved. There is a content to faith. Faith involves our minds.

As we nurture children in faith, we must teach them the truth about God, his Son and our need of redemption. Part of teaching children is communicating the truth, the content of the Christian faith. *What* a person believes is as important as *that* a person believes. If there is wrong content to belief, it is not Christian faith, but only false belief. Faith involves believing the right things, but faith is more than believing the right things.

The second part of faith has to do with our hearts. Faith is concerned with whom we love. Having faith in Jesus means loving him. He asked, "Peter, do you love me?" We cannot say that we have faith in Jesus if we do not love him. Jesus taught that the greatest commandments were to love God with all our hearts and to love our neighbor as ourselves. It is clear that believing has to do with loving.

Part of nurturing faith in children is teaching them to love God. Not only must we train their minds but we must also train their hearts. True faith delights in God and seeks after him. If a person has not learned to love God, that person does not have faith in the biblical sense. But faith involves more than our minds and our hearts. It also involves our wills.

The third part of faith has to do with the choices we make. Jesus said, "If you love me, you will obey what I command" (John 14:15). He clearly brought loving him and obeying him together. He insisted that if we claim to believe in him, we must obey his teaching. There is no belief apart from obedience.

Part of nurturing faith in children is teaching them to obey God. Unless they are choosing to be obedient to God, we cannot say they have faith. John wrote:

> We know that we have come to know him if we
> obey his commands. The man who says, "I know
> him," but does not do what he commands is a

liar, and the truth is not in him. But if anyone obeys his word, God's love is truly made complete in him. This is how we know we are in him: Whoever claims to live in him must walk as Jesus did (I John 2:3-6).

The faith that saves involves what we believe, whom we love and how we live. Belief in biblical perspective involves the whole person.

Historically, the term *belief* meant literally *by life*. Belief shaped the way a person lived. That idea is central to what it means to believe in Jesus. Nurturing faith in children means teaching them to live by the teachings of Jesus.

WHERE FAITH RESIDES

Nurturing faith in children means ministering to them spiritually. Meaningful interventions must include the spiritual needs of the child. But what is the *spiritual* aspect of the child and how do we minister spiritually?

The spiritual is not a separate entity within the person. Rather, it is the *essence* of what we are as human beings. There are five different aspects of human personhood, and each of these influences faith and the spiritual essence of the child. These are not aspects of faith but rather are the pathways through which spiritual ministry takes place.

An analogy can help us understand what persons are like. Just as the hand is made up of five fingers and a palm, so the human being is made up of five aspects, with the spiritual as the essence.

The first aspect is the physical. Human beings have physical bodies which need care. Sickness, hunger or injury will influence us spiritually. Meeting physical needs is many times the first step in spiritual nurture. Much of Jesus' ministry began with meeting the physical needs of those around him.

194

Figure 18:1 The hand analogy

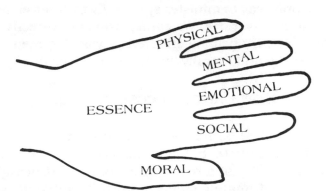

The second aspect of the human person is the mind. We are thinking beings who use ideas to understand and make sense of our world. Therefore part of faith is cognitive, having to do with what we believe. Teaching the truth is part of nurturing faith.

The third aspect is the emotional. Human beings are feeling beings, and the emotions are a powerful part of our personality. Faith has to do with receiving God's love and giving our love back in return. There is an emotional aspect to faith and an emotional ministry to children.

The fourth part of the human personality is the social. We are designed by God to relate to other persons. The idea of the church as the "body of Christ" is an emphasis on the relational part of being Christian. We are all part of a larger society and must learn to function in relationship to others. Christian nurture is always carried out in the context of relationships.

The final aspect is the moral. Human beings are designed by God to be concerned with questions of right and wrong and to behave in morally correct ways. Part of nurturing faith has to do with teaching children to behave in ways that God says are right.

The only way to minister spiritually to children is through one of these five avenues. We cannot minister directly from our spirits to theirs. By helping children physically, mentally, emotionally, socially and morally, we help them spiritually.

How children come to faith

True biblical faith is not something we can stir up ourselves. The ability to believe the gospel is a gift of God (Ephesians 2:8-9), not a result of human effort or right methods. Children ultimately come to faith because of God's love and mercy which draws them to him—not because we are good at working with them. Those who work with children must always see themselves as dependent upon God to bring children to faith. Therefore, this analysis is not offered as a formula for success but as a description of how God normally works with children.

Most children believe more with their hearts and wills than with their minds. They come to faith more through their emotions than through rational thought. Many times they develop the emotional part of faith before they develop the cognitive part.

Children respond to being loved. Emotionally, they are like little sponges, absorbing the love offered to them by adults. They will also respond emotionally when they are told of God's love. Even if they cannot understand it in rational ways, they may still understand it emotionally.

Jesus responded to little children, and they to him. He loved them, placing his hands upon them and blessing them. And the Bible teaches that the children responded to him in faith and in praise.

Especially children who have been harmed by events outside of their control need to be loved into the kingdom of God. They must be valued and respected, shown by how they are treated that they have dignity and worth. They must feel the love of God in the adults who work with them. Their first steps towards faith will be as they learn to respond to the love of the people around them.

Children who have physical needs, such as hunger, thirst, illness or pain, must first have these needs met. Feeding, clothing, providing medical attention will be the first steps towards nurturing them spiritually. Such actions must be understood as part of spiritual ministry to children. These are some of the pathways to nurturing faith.

But there must also be a content of faith taught to children. They must have some sense of *what* to believe about God and his Son, Jesus. As powerful as love is, love alone does not communicate the gospel. Children must also have a content to their belief.

Theologians differ on what is the absolute minimum a person can know and still be a Christian. It seems to me the heart of the gospel is that we are sinners who deserve punishment from God, but he has loved us and sent his Son, Jesus, to die in our place so that we might be forgiven. If we will believe in him in the sense described earlier, we can be redeemed and reconciled with God. This is the heart of the message that should be taught to children.

Children who come to faith will usually respond first emotionally to the love offered to them through adults who nurture them. When children feel safe and loved they will be willing to accept the truthfulness of the message the adults offer. They will believe the content of the gospel after they have felt the love of the gospel brought to them by adults. When we are willing to enter compassionately into the lives of the children, they will then be willing to believe our gospel.

GUIDELINES FOR NURTURING FAITH IN CHILDREN

Working with children has no ironclad guarantees. We are dependent upon God to reach them and bring them to faith. But given the characteristics of children, even those who have been the victims of severe abuse, the following guidelines seem especially helpful.

Treat children with respect

Children who have been abused and hurt by adults have not been shown respect. Dignity is not something that can be taken away from persons, but it is something that can be disregarded. When children are treated respectfully their dignity is being affirmed.

A primary need for children who hurt is to have their dignity affirmed. They must learn again that they have worth, and that they matter to adults and to God.

Great care must be taken to treat them respectfully. We must avoid manipulating them, or not taking seriously what has happened to them. It means loving them enough to let them speak of their anger, fear and distrust. It also may mean letting them be quiet, not forcing them to talk when they need to be silent.

Adults must lead the children. They are not equal partners with us. As children, they must be taught, led, disciplined and rebuked. But these actions must always be done in respect for the child as a person.

Teach them God's Word

Because there is a content to belief, children must be taught what to believe. We learn the content of faith from the Bible. There is no substitute for God's Word as the content of nurture. But the Bible must be taught in ways appropriate for children to understand. The apostle Paul wrote, "When I was a child, I talked like a child, I thought like a child, I reasoned like a child" (1 Corinthians 13:11). He recognized that children think differently from adults.

Children learn best through stories. Children everywhere love stories and they learn from them. The telling of stories is a time-honored means of teaching children, and of passing on information.

A large part of the Bible is story. The Old Testament especially, is filled with stories specifically designed to teach children. A primary way in which Israelites were to teach their children was through stories.

Effective nurturing of children is done through stories. Telling (not just reading) the stories of the Bible helps children understand who God is and the kinds of things he does. Children should be told the stories of the Bible as a means of learning about God and what he has done.

Some parts of the Bible are more direct in their style. Biblical commands on how we should behave towards self, God and others should also be taught. Children need to learn the commands of God, because these, too, are a gift of his grace.

God's commands are best taught in the context of life. If we set up a "school" and teach the Bible like we teach reading, the power of the Bible is lost. But if the commands are taught in relationship to everyday life, they have greater power and meaning.

The commands should be taught actively. The showing of kindness provides the context in which the command to be kind to one another can be taught. Acts of love provide the setting for teaching the commands to love one another. The commands of God are best taught as they are being lived out. In that way, the children can see them and feel them as well as hear them.

Model the truth in your life

Faith is best nurtured when it is being acted out in the life of the teacher. The apostle Paul wrote, "Whatever you have learned or received or heard from me or seen in me—put it into practice" (Philippians 4:9). He was aware that he was teaching by his life as well as by his lips.

Children learn a great deal by watching and by imitating. They observe adults to learn how to behave and imitate what they see in us. God has designed them to learn this way. Our task is to be good examples of what we are teaching.

If we treat others with disrespect, children will learn to be disrespectful from us. If we are rude, arrogant or proud, they will learn to be like that also. But if we model the fruit of the Spirit (Galatians 5:22-23), they will learn Christian behavior from our example.

The Bible regularly calls us to live lives worthy of the gospel. Part of the reason we must do this is to show children what it means to follow Jesus. They will learn from our example.

Traumatized children have had violence, inhumanity and wickedness modeled for them. They may be imitating these actions in their own lives. Our task is to model for them the more excellent way of love.

Modeling Christian faith for children does not mean that we must be perfect. Only God is perfect. We are called to be examples of redemption, not of perfection. We are all sinners being transformed into Christ's likeness—the process of redemption taking place in our lives. Children need to see God at work in us so they can understand how he will also be at work in them.

Modeling redemption requires honesty. We cannot pretend to be more spiritual than we really are. People (including children) know when we are not being honest. We must be willing to admit our faults and weaknesses, be willing to confess our sins and be willing to ask for forgiveness from those whom we have wronged. Modeling redemption does not mean being perfect. It means letting the process of God's work in the life of a sinner be seen in us.

It is most helpful if we will talk about the process that is going on in us with the children. Telling them how we are trying to obey God and ways in which we may be failing helps them understand what we are living out before them. Telling them what we are learning from the Bible and how we are trying to obey it makes the faith real to them. They will more quickly understand what it means to be a Christian if we talk with them about how it is being worked out in our own lives.

Being honest with others is a scary thing. It is especially scary to be honest with children. But part of respecting them is trusting them. When we are willing to tell them about our own struggles and pain, they will be more willing to tell us about theirs.

Enter into relationship with them and love them

One of the keys to Jesus' ministry was that he loved people. They were receptive to his message because he loved them. When he reached out in compassion to the lepers, and *touched* them, they knew that his message was authentic. No one else ever touched a leper, but Jesus showed that he loved them by his touch.

Children who have been abused will be afraid of relationships. They will know neither how to give nor how to receive love. It will be up to the adult to break down the barriers to enter into relationship with them.

The gospel of God's love must be accompanied with compassion. Jesus taught that we must "be merciful, just as your Father is merciful" (Luke 6:36). We must treat others in the same way that God has treated us.

We cannot give a true gift of love without a gift of ourselves. We must be willing to give ourselves in love to the children we wish to nurture. We must become a living expression of the gospel by loving them just as God has loved us.

It is a dangerous thing to love children. If they respond, they will become dependent upon us and will attach themselves emotionally to us. Their need to be loved will drive them to us in demanding and draining ways. But such is the ministry of love.

Children who respond to love will want to test the reality of our love. They will test and try us in amazing ways, all to be sure that we really do love them. Part of their testing will be to push the limits of acceptable behavior. Our love must be tough. We must be willing to confront and correct the children as part of our love, just as God corrects us. They will want to know if we love them enough to stop them from doing wrong.

Nurturing faith will involve tough love. The child must be told, "Because I love you, I cannot allow you to behave in this way." The language of love is sometimes the language of confrontation.

Loving children involves a great cost. Your heart will be broken by them, and the emotional pain can be intense. We must understand that suffering is part of ministry. The apostle Paul wrote, "I want to know Christ and the power of his resurrection and the fellowship of sharing in his sufferings, becoming like him in his death . . ." (Philippians 3:10). Part of following Christ for Paul was to share in the fellowship of Christ's sufferings.

Abused children have experienced the horror of adult hatred and violence. To be nurtured in the faith, they must also experience the power of unselfish love. Such love comes with a price; it costs the person who gives it. To nurture faith in children will require that we be willing to love them enough to bear the pain of emotional commitment to them.

The power to do this well resides in our relationship with God. John tells us:

> Jesus knew that the Father had put all things under his power, and that he had come from God and was returning to God; so he got up from the meal, took off his outer clothing, and wrapped a towel around his waist. After that, he poured water into a basin and began to wash his disciples' feet, drying them with the towel that was wrapped around him (John 13:3-5).

Jesus was free to take the role of a servant (even to the point of death) because he understood his relationship to God. The sustaining power to minister to hurting children must come from our relationship to the Father, and our understanding of who we are before him.

Pray for the children

The battle for these children may be political, psychological, physical or militaristic. But in the final analysis, it is spiritual. The forces of God are in battle with the forces of evil, and wickedness fills the hearts of many. The apostle Paul wrote:

> Put on the full armor of God so that you can take your stand against the devil's schemes. For our

struggle is not against flesh and blood, but against the rulers, against the authorities, against the powers of this dark world and against the spiritual forces of evil in the heavenly realms (Ephesians 6:11–12).

If all we have to reach these children is our own power, the work is hopeless. They will be lost to any possibility of redemption to useful lives. But God invites us to prayer, promising that he will hear and respond. Our ultimate power is in asking God to heal these children; to use our efforts as expressions of his love and redemption.

For those who minister, prayer is a resource which we dare not ignore. The heart of our Lord's teaching was that God loves us and listens to us when we pray. Because of the character of God, who loves these children more than we do, we can ask him to heal them, to draw them to himself and to give them faith. David wrote, ". . . ,You have set your glory above the heavens. From the lips of children and infants you have ordained praise because of your enemies, to silence the foe and the avenger" (Psalm 8:1-2). We may ask our Father to put praise on the lips of these children as he has ordained, and their praise will be the victory over the enemies.

Because of God, it is possible to see lives redeemed from destruction. It is not because we are so good at working with children but because God is more powerful than the forces of evil that have been brought against them. We can ask God, and he can prevail in the lives of the children.

18

God's Heart for the Fatherless

Edward T. Bradley

James tell us "religion that God our Father accepts as pure and faultless is this: to look after orphans and widows in their distress and to keep oneself from being polluted by the world" (1:27). If James is right, Mary Edeh Ojomo is the most religious woman I know.

When Mary was growing up in a remote Nigerian village, her mother lived out the gospel in a way no one else in the community ever had. In Mary's culture, where every able body is needed to help farm or work around the home, crippled or handicapped children are deemed worthless. They are abandoned to live, or die, in the street. Mary's mother, out of compassion for these helpless, abandoned children, defied the traditions of her people and took in as many as her tiny house would hold. As God stretched the oil for the widow (2 Kings 4:1–7), Mary's mother saw food, clothing—and love—stretched beyond human means. Since Mary's mother died, her heart for the fatherless lives on through her daughter. Mary now runs a school and orphanage in her village.

Mary's reputation has spread so far that one day last year a taxi roared into the village—one of the few cars to traverse the dusty, rocky trails—and stopped in front of Mary's school.

The driver stepped out of the car, opened the passenger door, picked up a small, wriggling bundle and hurriedly deposited it in Mary's arms. Mary glimpsed inside to see a tiny, handicapped child. "I heard you care for these babies and I'm handing it to you. If you won't take it, I'm throwing it out in the street." Without another word, the driver stepped back into the taxi and took off for the city. Mary never saw the man again, never knew the baby's name or birthplace, but she never allowed that child to be abandoned again.

Sadly, in today's world Mary is considered a unique individual, singled out for a special calling or ministry to orphans just as others have a ministry to high school students, internationals or prisoners. Yet, throughout the Old and New Testaments we see God the Father and Jesus pleading on behalf of the fatherless and others who are powerless, helpless and utterly dependent upon him—or upon his people. His compassion compels and commands us to care for them, to have his heart for them and to share in the responsibility of that care.

God's desire for the fatherless

In the Old Testament, the fatherless are frequently grouped with the widows and aliens. God reveals his heart for the fatherless and exhibits the characteristics of a loving Father toward them as he offers them protection, provides for their food and other necessities, and requires justice for them in society.

The Old Testament law

Three Old Testament passages demonstrate this desire of the Father.

1. In Exodus 22:22–24 God admonishes the Israelites not to take advantage of a widow or an orphan. He makes a promise that should this command be broken, he will certainly hear the cry of the widow and

orphan. He will respond by bringing down judgment on the offenders, killing them with the sword and leaving their children fatherless and their wives widowed. In effect, he reverses the roles of the helpless and the empowered.

2. God desires for the have-nots—those who have nothing through no fault of their own—to eat and be satisfied (Deuteronomy 14:28–29). At the end of every three years the Israelites were to gather a tithe from that year's produce and donate it to a storage facility in the town, so the Levites, aliens, fatherless and widows who lived there could come, eat and be satisfied. He made a promise to the have-nots to sustain them in their time of need and promised the "haves" to bless them in all the work of their hands. What a "win-win" situation!

3. Justice is another of God's requirements for all but particularly for the powerless. "Do not deprive the alien or the fatherless of justice, or take the cloak of the widow as a pledge," says Deuteronomy 24:17. When he laid down the law to the Israelites, God gave them a very real reminder of why they were to follow his command—because he had done the same for them not so long before. "Remember that you were slaves in Egypt and the Lord your God redeemed you from there. That is why I command you to do this" (24:18). And what if they failed to render justice? God's judgment was clear: "Woe to those who make unjust laws, to those who issue oppressive decrees, to deprive the poor of their rights and withhold justice from the oppressed of my people, making widows their prey and robbing the fatherless" (Isaiah 10:1–2). "Cursed is the man who withholds justice from the alien, the fatherless or the widow" (Deuteronomy 27:19).

It's interesting to note how God measured his people's love for him by society's treatment of the fatherless and widows. In the Old Testament, a sure sign that God's people were in a state of rebellion and spiritual anarchy came through when they neglected the widows and fatherless. Ezekiel 22:6–7,12 refers to the princes of Israel: "In you they have treated father and mother with contempt; in you they have oppressed the alien and mistreated the fatherless and the widow . . . . And you have forgotten me, declares the Sovereign Lord." Malachi 3:5 issues this warning from the Lord Almighty: "So I will come near to you for judgment. I will be quick to testify against sorcerers, adulterers and perjurers, against those who defraud laborers of their wages, who oppress the widows and the fatherless, and deprive aliens of justice, but do not fear me." In other words, they had abandoned the true religion, of which James would speak hundreds of years later, for the pollution of the world.

Throughout the Old Testament, God revealed his heart for the poor through his laws and decrees. He demanded from his people the same compassion, justice and provision for the fatherless that he had shown as their Heavenly Father when he brought them out of oppression.

Jesus, the New Testament model

While the Old Testament "modeled" God's character and nature through the revelation of his Law, the New Testament gives us the ultimate role model, Jesus. Jesus was the incarnation of the attributes and character of his Heavenly Father.

Perhaps the most familiar example of Christ's love for the children is related in the Gospel of Mark, when they are brought to him for his blessing (Mark 10:13–16). Jesus and the disciples had been traveling from town to town for days, preaching, teaching and healing. Everywhere they went large crowds followed, pushing in on Jesus, calling out to him, asking difficult questions and sometimes not liking the answers they received. Jesus must have been exhausted and most likely at a point where solitude and quiet would have been a welcome respite. But toward the end of an incredibly busy day, instead of slipping away with two or three of his best friends for a quiet evening, Jesus responded to the group of parents who approached him with their young children in tow, all asking for his touch or blessing.

The practice of the day was to bring children from infancy to 12 years old to the elders or scribes for a prayer of blessing upon them on the evening of the Day of Atonement. So, here they all were, gathering around Jesus—not for healing or teaching but for his "touch," his blessing upon them. Yet, when the children neared Jesus the disciples sharply rebuked them. I can almost see Peter now, short of temper after a long day and protective of his Master. I can almost hear his thoughts: "Who do they think they are, bothering us after all the important work we've accomplished today? Can't they see Jesus is tired and has better ways to spend his evening?" Obviously, the disciples considered the children rather unimportant and a low priority in Jesus' heavy schedule.

But Jesus had his priorities ordered differently. In fact, instead of rebuking the parents and children, he rebuked the disciples! Verse 14 says Jesus was "indignant." The Greek word here, meaning "to grieve much," occurs only this once in the entire New Testament. In other words, Jesus went ballistic! his response to the disciples was proactive and forceful: "Let the little children come to me, and do not hinder them, for the kingdom of God belongs to such as these." His response to the children was much more tender—he opened his arms wide, beckoned the children to come, scooped them up, put his hands on them and blessed them. What a contrast! Food for thought: the things which grieve us or make us indignant reveal much about the kind of people we are. With whom do you most identify, Peter or Jesus?

While this is the most striking example of Christ's compassion for children, we see it displayed time and again in the imagery he chooses to illustrate his teachings. He celebrates the delight of a mother on giving birth to a child (John 16:21) and affirms the parental love which listens to a child's every request (Luke 11:11). Many of Jesus' miracles involved children as well: the healing of the royal official's son (John 4:46–54), the demonized "only son" of the man at the Mount of Transfiguration (Mark 9:14–29) and Jarius' 12-year-old daughter (Luke 8).

Such attention paid by Jesus to those whom the society of his day deemed powerless, worthless and unimportant was remarkable and yet another indication of his and his Father's heart for the fatherless. It's also an indication of his loving plan for us, for he teaches us a valuable spiritual lesson through his dealings with children. Let's return again for a moment to the passage in Mark 10. When Jesus rebukes the disciples, he reminds them that "the kingdom of God belongs to such as these. I tell you the truth," he continues, "anyone who will not receive the kingdom of God like a little child will never enter it." Notice the emphasis placed on the words "not" and "never." No one will get into the kingdom of God unless he or she receives God's salvation like a child—NOT ONE!

Children are role models for us to enter the kingdom of God. But what does this analogy mean? We can't infer innocence: we don't enter the kingdom of God because we are innocent babies. It doesn't imply subjective attitudes such as trustfulness, receptivity or simplicity. It means we enter the kingdom of God when we see ourselves in relationship to him as little children see themselves in relationship to a father—utterly helpless, dependent, bankrupt beings in need of a compassionate, protecting, sustaining, just Heavenly Father.

Through the Mark 10 passage we gain insight into what we receive from God when we enter the kingdom as those children. When the children came to Jesus they were met with open arms, they were embraced and they received his blessing. Here a prefix is added to the Greek word for bless which intensifies the force of the word to "blessed fervently." Jesus prays for his children with great gusto!

What an incredible picture of our Heavenly Father's love for us, his adopted children! As we come to him, fatherless, helpless and utterly dependent upon him, he opens his arms wide, embraces us and blesses us—with great gusto!

As his children and followers, we are commanded to embody this aspect of his character. The Israelites were commanded to care for the orphans and widows because they had been brought out of slavery and redeemed by God. We are to respond in the same way because we have been brought out of spiritual slavery and redeemed by our Heavenly Father.

George MacDonald once said that he doubted a man's Christianity if children were never found playing around his door. While you may not have a passel of kids playing with Pogs on your doorstep or have a taxi driver drop a bundle into your arms, you have the privilege and the responsibility of modeling God's heart for the fatherless to future generations. According to the Orphan Foundation of America, there are more than 10 million orphans in the United States. The World Health Organization (WHO) estimates that in late 1993 about 2.5 million children, 90 percent of them in Africa, had lost one or both parents to AIDS. Worldwide wars have orphaned countless children. The rise in single parent homes in America has left hundreds of thousands of children fatherless.

Be a man or woman after God's heart. Run to him with open arms and allow him to embrace you and bless you. Then turn around and live out the instruction of James 1:27 "to look after orphans and widows in their distress." God our Father accepts this kind of religion as pure and faultless.

19

The Spiritual Battle for Children

Neil T. Anderson

I have had the privilege of helping thousands of Christians find their freedom in Christ over the last several years. Most of them have been Christian leaders, their spouses or their children. In most cases their problems originated when they were children. Many parents believe that a Christian home, an active church and a Christian school will insulate and protect their children from the world, the flesh and the devil. In reality, those families are often the targets of the powers of darkness who are seeking to destroy their homes and their ministries. In preparation for writing *The Seduction Of Our Children*, Steve Russo and I researched over 1700 professing Christian teenagers.

The following results are what we found in one thoroughly evangelical Christian high school:[1]

- Forty-five percent said they have experienced a "presence" (seen or heard) in their room that scared them.
- Fifty-nine percent said they've harbored bad thoughts about God.
- Forty-three percent said they find it mentally hard to pray and read their Bible.

- Sixty-nine percent reported hearing "voices" in their head, like there was a subconscious voice talking to them.
- Twenty-two percent said they frequently entertain thoughts of suicide.
- Seventy-four percent think they are different from others. (It works for others but not for them).

As bad as those percentages are, they rise considerably if children have dabbled in the occult, followed counterfeit guidance or played certain fantasy games that no Christian should be playing. How do we explain that seven out of ten of our professing Christian young people are hearing "voices"? Are they paranoid, schizophrenic or psychotic? I don't believe that. I believe 1 Timothy 4:1: "The Spirit clearly says that in later times some will abandon the faith and follow deceiving spirits and things taught by demons."

Is that happening? It's happening all over the world. Let me offer some explanation for the spiritual battle we are all in by looking at a portion of the high priestly prayer in John 17:13-20:

> I am coming to you now, but I say these things while I am still in the world, so that they may have the full measure of my joy within them. I have given them your word and the world has hated them, for they are not of the world any more than I am of the world. My prayer is not that you take them out of the world but that you protect them from the evil one. They are not of the world, even as I am not of it. Sanctify them by the truth; your word is truth. As you sent me into the world, I have sent them into the world. For them I sanctify myself, that they too may be truly sanctified. My prayer is not for them alone. I pray also for those who will believe in me through their message.

That we be kept from the evil one is the concern Jesus has for his disciples and for all those who believe in him. He is returning to the Father, but the disciples and the soon-to-be-established church are going to remain on Planet Earth where "the prince of this world" (John 14:30), "the ruler of the kingdom of the air" (Ephesians 2:2) and "your enemy the devil prowls around like a roaring lion looking for someone to devour" (1 Peter 5:8). Unlike concerned parents who may be tempted to isolate their children from the harsh realities of this world, Jesus didn't ask that we be removed. That strategy would result in no growth for the children or the church and thus no future ministry. His prayer is that we be protected from the evil one.

Scary thought, but he has not left us or our children defenseless. First, "you have been given fullness in Christ, who is the head over every power and authority" (Colossians 2:10). Christians are established in Christ and seated with him in the heavenly realms (Ephesians 2:6). Because of our position in Christ, we have all the authority we need over the evil one to carry out the delegated responsibility of fulfilling the Great Commission (Matthew 28:18-20). Second, "having disarmed the powers and authorities, he made a public spectacle of them, triumphing over them by the cross" (Colossians 2:15). "His intent was that now, through the church, the manifold wisdom of God should be made known to the rulers and authorities in the heavenly realms, according to his eternal purpose which he accomplished in Christ Jesus our Lord" (Ephesians 3:10-11).

Paul is stating the eternal purpose of God which is to make his wisdom known through the church. To whom? To the rulers and authorities in the heavenly realm, that is the spiritual realm. "The Son of God appeared for this *purpose*, that He might destroy the works of the devil" (1 John 3:8, NASB emphasis added). If the battle is between the kingdom of darkness and the kingdom of light, between the Christ and the anti-Christ, and God's eternal purpose is to make his wisdom known through the church to the rulers and authorities, how are we doing?

Not very well I'm afraid. Half the "church" doesn't even believe in a personal devil, which has always been a standard doctrine of the historical Christian church. Most operate as though he doesn't exist, having little understanding how the spiritual world impinges on ourselves or our families. A few would even insist that there is no interaction. Others make a conscious choice not to deal with the reality of the devil out of fear. In some circles it isn't academically credible. Many of us, like blindfolded warriors, don't know who our enemy is, so we strike out at ourselves and each other.

As we confront this hostile world, the Lord has not left us defenseless. We have a sanctuary in Christ, and he has equipped us with the armor of God. We have all the resources we need in Christ to stand firm and resist the devil, but if we don't assume our responsibility those resources will go unused. He has instructed us to put on the armor of God. What if we haven't? We have been told to "put on the Lord Jesus Christ, and make no provision for the flesh in regard to its lusts" (Romans 13:14 NASB). What if we have made provision for the flesh? We are told to submit to God and resist the devil (James 4:7). What if we don't? God's provision for our freedom in Christ is limited only to the degree that we fail to recognize our position in Christ and assume our responsibility.

The most common and naive response in the Western world is to ignore the battle or make the fatal assumption that Christians are somehow immune. Just the opposite is true. Ignorance is not bliss; it's defeat. If you are a Christian, you're the target. If you are a pastor, you and your family are the bull's eye. It is the strategy of Satan to render Christians inoperative and to obliterate the truth that we are "dead to sin, but alive to God in Christ Jesus" (Romans 6:11).

The divorce rate and disintegration of the Christian family roughly parallels the secular world. The distinction between a Christian and a pagan is no longer obvious. Even the tragic fall of many visible Christian leaders indicates that something is dreadfully wrong. Having an intellectual knowledge of Scripture obviously isn't enough, because I'm sure these leaders had such knowledge. "Christianity doesn't work" is the mistaken message many are choosing to believe.

If you are tempted to think that you are spiritually immune to the attacks of the evil one, let me ask you three pertinent questions. First, have you experienced any temptation this week? Biblically, who is the tempter? It can't be God. He will test our faith to strengthen it, but Satan's temptations are intended to destroy our faith. Second, have you ever struggled with the voice of the accuser of the brethren? Before you answer, let me ask the question in another way. Have you ever struggled with thoughts like, "I'm stupid," or "I'm ugly," or "I can't," or "God doesn't love me," or "I'm different from others," or "I'm going down"? I know you have, because the Bible says that Satan accuses the brethren day and night. Third, have you ever been deceived? The person who is tempted to answer no may be the most deceived of all.

ASSESSING THE BATTLE

Let me share with you what I think is the real battle. If I tempt you; you know it. If I accuse you; you will know it. But if I deceive you; you don't know it. If you knew it, you would no longer be deceived. Now listen to the logic of Scripture: "If you hold to my teaching, you are really my disciples. Then you will know the truth, and the truth will set you free" (John 8:31-32). Jesus answered, "I am the way and the truth and the life" (John 14:6). In the high priestly prayer, Jesus prayed, "Sanctify them by the truth; your word is truth" (John 17:17). When we put on the armor of God, the first thing we do is put on the "belt of truth" (Ephesians 6:14).

What was the conflict that required God to intervene dramatically in the early church when he struck down Ananias and Sapphira? Peter asked, "Ananias, how is it that Satan has so filled your heart that you have lied to the Holy Spirit and have kept for yourself some of the money you received for the land?" (Acts 5:3-4). The message couldn't have been made more clear. If Satan can operate undetected in your church, your home, your marriage or you, and get you to believe a lie, could he control your life? The Lord had to expose the battle for the mind as soon as Satan raised his ugly head in the early church. That strategy is not new. Satan deceived Ananias and Sapphira to lie to the Holy Spirit. Satan also *deceived* Eve, and she believed a *lie*.

Why don't we know this? For one reason, I can't read your mind, and you can't read my mind. So we really don't have any idea what is going on in the minds of other people unless they have the courage to share with us. In many cases they won't, because in our culture many people will wrongly assume that you are mentally ill. They will tell you about their abuse or what has happened to them, but only to the right person would they dare share what is going on inside. Are they mentally ill, or is there a battle going on for their minds? The lack of any balanced biblical contribution to mental health professions has left them with only one conclusion. Any problem in the mind must either be psychological or neurological.

A common medical explanation for those who hear voices, have panic attacks, suffer from severe depression or see things in their room is, "You have a chemical imbalance." Chances are that a prescription for medication will be given with the hope of curing the problem or eliminating the symptoms. I believe that our body chemistry can get out of balance and cause discomfort, and hormonal problems can throw our systems off. But I also believe that other legitimate questions need to be asked, such as, "How can a chemical produce a personal thought?" and "How can our neurotransmitters involuntarily and randomly fire in such a way to create thoughts we are opposed to thinking?" Is there a natural explanation for that? I'm willing to hear any legitimate answers and explanations, because I really care for people. I want to see their problems resolved by the grace of God, but I don't think that will happen unless we take into account the reality of the spiritual world.

When people say they are hearing voices, what are they actually hearing? The only way we can physically hear with our ears is to have a sound source that compresses air molecules. Sound waves move through the physical medium of air and strike our ear drums which send a signal to our brains. That is how we physically hear. But the "voices" that people hear, or the "thoughts" that they struggle with are not coming from that kind of source.

In a similar fashion, when people say they see things (that others don't), what are they actually seeing? The only way we can naturally see something is to have a light source reflecting off a material object back to our eyes which sends a signal to our brain. Satan and his demons are spiritual beings; they do not have material substance, so we cannot see a spiritual being with our natural eyes, nor hear them with our ears. "For our struggle is not against flesh and blood, but against the rulers, against the authorities, against the powers of this dark world and against the spiritual forces of evil in the heavenly realms" (Ephesians 6:12).

FIGHTING THE BATTLE

What do typical parents do when a frightened child comes into their bedroom and claims to have seen or heard something in his or her room? They will probably go into the child's room, look in the closet or under the bed and say, "There is nothing in your room, Honey, now go back to sleep!" If you are an adult and you saw something in your room would you just forget about it and go back to sleep? "But I looked in the room. There was nothing there," you respond. There never was anything in the room that could be observed by our natural senses. "Then it isn't real," says the skeptic. Oh yes it is! What that child saw or heard was in his or her own mind, and it was very real.

I can't explain how people pay attention to deceiving spirits. I don't know how the devil does it, but I don't have to know how he does it to believe what Scripture clearly teaches. The spiritual battle for our minds does not operate according to the laws of nature. No physical barriers can confine or restrict the movements of Satan. The frightened face of a child testifies that the battle is real. Why not respond to your child as follows:

Honey, I believe that you saw or heard something. I didn't hear or see anything so that helps me understand that you are under spiritual attack. Before I pray for your protection, I want you to know that Jesus is much bigger and more powerful than anything you see or hear that frightens you. The Bible teaches us that Jesus living in us is greater than any monsters in the world. Because Jesus is always with us, we can tell whatever is frightening us to leave in Jesus' name. The Bible tells us to submit to God and resist the devil and he will flee from us. Can you do that, Honey? Do you have any questions? Then let's pray together.

There is much we don't know about mental functioning, but we do know that a fundamental difference exists between our brains and our minds. Our brains are organic matter. When we die physically, we separate from our bodies, and our brains return to dust. At that moment, we will be absent from our bodies and present with the Lord. But we won't be mindless, because the mind is a part of the soul. Our ability to think is similar to the way a computer functions. Both have two separate components: one is the hardware, which is the actual physical computer (brain); the other is the software (mind), which programs the hardware. If the software is removed from the hardware it would weigh the same. Likewise, if the Spirit is removed from the body, it would also remain the same weight. A computer is totally worthless without the software, but the software won't work either if the hardware shuts down.

Our society assumes that if something is not functioning right between the ears it must be a hardware problem. I don't believe the primary problem is the hardware; I think the primary problem is the software. If a person has organic brain syndrome, Down's syndrome or Alzheimer's disease, the brain won't function very well. Severe brain damage, however, is relatively rare, and little can be done about it. Romans 12:1-2 says we are to submit our bodies to God (which includes the brain) and be transformed by the renewing of our minds.

Much of what is being passed off today as mental illness is nothing more than a battle for our minds. Proverbs 23:7 (NASB) says, "For as he thinks within himself, so he is." In other words, you don't do anything without first thinking it. All behavior is the product of what we choose to think or believe. We can't see what people think. We can only observe what they do. So when our children misbehave we try to change their behavior, but we should be trying to understand what they are thinking and change what they believe.

CHILDREN ARE PRIME TARGETS

Since we can't read another person's mind, we have to learn to ask the right questions. In *The Seduction Of Our Children* I shared the story of five-year-old Danny who was sent to the office of his Christian school for hurting several other children on the playground. He had been acting aggressively toward others and was restless in class. His teacher said, "I'm puzzled by his recent behavior. It isn't like Danny to act this way!" Danny's mother was a teacher at the school. When she asked her son about Jesus, he covered his ears and shouted, "I hate Jesus!" Then he grasped his mother and laughed in a hideous voice!

I asked Danny if he ever heard voices talking to him in his head. He looked relieved at the question and volunteered that voices were shouting at him on the playground to hurt other kids. The thoughts were so loud that the only way to quiet them was to obey, even though he knew he would get into trouble. We told Danny that he didn't have to listen to the voices anymore. We led Danny through the children's version of the "Steps To Freedom" (see appendix B), having him pray the prayers after us. When we were finished we asked him how he felt. A big smile came on his face, and with a sigh of relief he said, "Much better!" His teacher noticed a calmness the next day as though he were a different child. He has not repeated his aggressive behavior in school.

A committed Christian couple adopted a young boy and received him into their home with open arms before he was five. Their innocent little boy turned into a monster. Their home was in turmoil when I was asked to talk to him. After some friendly chatter I asked him if it ever seemed like someone was talking to him in his head. "Yes," he said, "All the time."

"What are they saying," I asked.

"They're telling me that I'm no good."

I asked him if he ever asked Jesus into his life. He said, "Yes, but I didn't mean it." I told him that if he really did ask Jesus to come into his life he could tell those voices to leave him. Realizing that truth, he gave his heart to Christ.

Another committed couple heard thumping on the wall of their son's room. He had taken a pair of scissors and stabbed the wall several times. They never caught him doing the act nor found the scissors. Then the child began to cut up every piece of clothing in the house. Again they never caught their son actually doing the cutting. Huge medical and counseling bills piled up as they desperately tried to find a solution. Finally the parents were introduced to our material and began to consider the possibility of this problem being spiritual. So they asked their son if he ever had thoughts telling him to do what he was doing. He said, "Yes, and if I didn't do what they told me to do, they said they would kill you [the father]!" The little boy thought he was saving his father's life. I have heard that response more than once.

JESUS THE ULTIMATE ANSWER

To get a better understanding of what we are dealing with, let's look at the bigger picture. Before we came to Christ we had neither the presence of God in our lives, nor the knowledge of his ways. Consequently, we learned to live our lives independent of God. When we committed our lives to the Lord and were born again we became new creations in Christ. The good news is that salvation comes with a brand-new software package. The bad news is that there's no delete button, so the old software (flesh or old nature) is still loaded into the memory bank and the computer is vulnerable to viruses (the fiery darts of the evil one). We have to consciously choose to renew (re-program) our minds and constantly check for viruses (demonic attacks). Paul says:

> For though we live in the world, we do not wage war as the world does. The weapons we fight with are not the weapons of the world. On the contrary, they have divine power to demolish strong-holds. We demolish arguments and every pre-tension that sets itself up against the knowledge of God, and we take captive every thought to make it obedient to Christ (2 Corinthians 10:3-5).

Every child of God must assume responsibility to choose the truth and to teach the children to do likewise.

I have a great respect for the medical profession, and I think the church should work hand in glove with committed doctors. Taking a pill to cure your body is commendable, but taking a pill to cure your soul is deplorable. Every legitimate doctor knows that the medical model can take you only so far. The most conservative estimate by the medical profession is that fifty percent of their patients are there because of psycho-somatic reasons. Who has the answer for that? The secular world that has no knowledge of God? We shouldn't be intimi-dated as though the church has no valid contribution. The church is "the pillar and foundation of the truth" (1 Timothy 3:15), and it is that truth that will set our people, including children, free.

Please don't assume that I think all our problems are spiritual, because I don't believe that. I do believe that we must have a whole answer for a whole person. The church has to be careful not to think that there is a "spiritual" answer for every-thing. For the same reason the medical profession must not assume a "physical" answer for everything. We need each other because we are both physical and spiritual beings who live in both a physical and a spiritual world, and God created both.

I'm often asked how I know whether a person's problem is spiritual or psychological. I believe that is the wrong question, and forces us into a false dichotomy. Our problems never are not psychological. At no time are our minds, wills and emotions not involved or pertinent to the situation. Our humanity is never in doubt this side of eternity. On the other hand, our problems never are not spiritual. At no time is God not here or irrelevant. He is right now "sustaining all things by his powerful word" (Hebrews 1:3). To my knowledge, there is no time when it is safe to take off the armor of God. The possibility of being tempted, accused or deceived is a continuous reality.

Actually the Bible teaches that the unseen world is more real than the seen world, "For what is seen is temporary, but what is unseen is eternal" (2 Corinthians 4:18). If we could just accept that fact, we would stop polarizing into psychotherapeutic ministries [various forms of mental treatment] that ignore the reality of the spiritual world, or jump into some kind of deliverance ministry that ignores developmental issues and human responsibility. Neither extreme can adequately provide a comprehensive answer. We must take into account all of reality, and strive for a balanced message.

Basically the answer is "Submit yourselves, then, to God. Resist the devil, and he will flee from you" (James 4:7). Trying to resist the devil without first submitting to God will result in a dog fight. That is often the error of confrontational type deliverance ministries. On the other hand, you can submit to God without resisting the devil, and stay in bondage. The tragedy of our time, is that many recovery ministries aren't doing either one. Submitting to God requires us to deal with the sin in our lives. Sin is like garbage, it attracts flies. So get rid of the flies, right? Wrong! Get rid of the garbage. If you get rid of the garbage, the flies will have no reason (right) to be there.

THE TRUTH ENCOUNTER

I didn't ask for my first encounter with the powers of darkness: it was thrust upon me. My feeble attempt was based on the most commonly perceived process of calling up the demon, getting its name and rank and then casting it out. I found the process ugly, exhausting and potentially harmful to the victim. Often the process had to be repeated, and the results didn't seem to last. In this procedure the deliverer seems to be the pastor, counselor or missionary. The information is gotten from the demons. Why would you believe them? We are clearly told that "there is no truth in him. When he lies, he speaks his native language, for he is a liar and the father of lies" (John 8:44).

I also found the process not very transferable. The procedure is often based on giftedness or an office of the church. I think there is a better and much more transferable procedure. I believe Jesus is the deliverer, and he has already come. Second, we should get our information from the Holy Spirit because he is "the Spirit of truth," and "he will guide you into all truth" (John 16:13).

The shifting of my thinking began when I realized that it was truth that set us free, and Jesus is the truth. His prayer in John 17 is that we be kept from the evil one by being sanctified in the word of God which is the truth. That is why I prefer to think of our battle as more of a truth encounter as opposed to a power encounter. I know of no place in the Bible that instructs us to seek power. The reason is we already have all the power we need because of our incredible position in Christ. Paul wrote:

> I pray also that the eyes of your heart may be enlightened in order that you may know the hope to which he has called you, the riches of his glorious inheritance in the saints, and his incomparably great power for us who believe. That power is like the working of his mighty strength,

which he exerted in Christ when he raised him
from the dead . . . (Ephesians 1:18-20).

The power for Christians lies in their ability to believe
the truth, and the power of the evil one is in his ability to
deceive. When you expose the lie, his power is broken. Often
when Christians struggle, they wrongly conclude that they lack
power. The temptation is to pursue some experience that will
give them more power. It will be a false trip. Satanists pursue
power, because it has been stripped from them. Christians
pursue the truth.

I don't think anyone in full time ministry seeks an encounter with the powers of darkness. But, whether they like it
or not, such encounters come with the ministry. With a little
experience and an honest search of Scripture, you will discover, as I did, that truth sets people free and each person has
to assume responsibility to resolve his or her personal and
spiritual conflicts. I can't fight your fight for you, or believe for
you or confess for you, but I can help you as Paul outlines in
the pastoral epistle, 2 Timothy 2:24-26:

> And the Lord's servant must not quarrel; instead,
> he must be kind to everyone, able to teach, not
> resentful. Those who oppose him he must gently
> instruct, in the hope that God will grant repen-
> tance leading them to a knowledge of the truth,
> and that they will come to their senses and es-
> cape from the trap of the devil, who has taken
> them captive to do his will.

This is not a power model, it is a kind, compassionate
and able-to-teach model. It requires a dependency upon the
Lord, for only he can grant the repentance which gets rid of
the garbage. It identifies truth as the liberating agent, and
implies that the battle is for the mind. It is totally transferable,
because all it requires is a lovingly mature bondservant of the
Lord who knows the truth. I know the latter is true because

we have had the privilege to train thousands of pastors, missionaries and lay people all over the world who are at this time setting captives free in Christ. And I deeply believe that everyone can be equipped to protect and help children.

Does Christ want us free? Of course! "It is for freedom that Christ has set us free. Stand firm, then, and do not let yourselves be burdened again by a yoke of slavery" (Galatians 5:1). The context of this verse is freedom from the law. Legalism is a bondage in and of itself. The answer for you and your family is not to just lay down the law. Should you be tempted to throw off all legal or moral constraints and go too far in the other direction, then consider Galatians 5:13 "You, my brothers, were called to be free. But do not use your freedom to indulge the sinful nature, . . . "

The "Steps to Freedom" which I developed are just a tool to help people resolve the issues that are critical between themselves and God, and then resist the devil. You couldn't hurt anybody with the process unless you created some false hope. The worst thing that could happen by going through the "Steps To Freedom" is this: you would really be ready for communion the next Sunday. In the process we are trying to help people resolve their personal and spiritual conflicts so that the life of Christ will be manifested in them. Then they can do all things through Christ who strengthens them.

Paul says, "But I am afraid that just as Eve was deceived by the serpent's cunning, your minds may somehow be led astray from your sincere and pure devotion to Christ" (2 Corinthians 11:3). I share the same concern for every child of God. My desire is to see all Christians live their lives free in Christ, which is their spiritual birthright. And I desire to see every marriage, family and ministry alive in Christ and free to be all that God has called them to be. Jesus is the answer, and his truth will set you and your family free. He is the Bondage Breaker.

NOTES

[1] Neil T. Anderson, Steve Russo, *The Seduction of Our Children* (Eugene, Oregon: Harvest House, 1991), p. 33.

20

Toward A Biblical Theology of Suffering

Warren Heard

In the Bible the issue of suffering, especially the suffering of the innocent, never is answered fully. Nevertheless, a number of explanations given by Scripture help us to answer the questions surrounding suffering.

- Where is God when the innocent suffer?
- Why does God let innocent people suffer?
- What is God trying to teach us? and finally,
- What is the Christian's role in ministering to those who suffer?

Scripture gives many reasons for suffering—reasons that demonstrate the extent to which the people of God struggled with the question of suffering. At difficult times each of the different explanations made sense. Since similar conditions exist today as they did in biblical history, all of these explanations are, at times, relevant.

It may be helpful, therefore, to summarize briefly several of the biblical explanations of suffering, though at no point is it being suggested that any of these interpretations are mutually exclusive. In light of the number of interpretations within the Bible itself, it is very probable that God's people embraced many explanations simultaneously to explain their current situation of suffering. Therefore, for Christian workers in an area where the suffering of innocent people, especially children, is widespread, it is hoped that some of the following definitions and explanations may equip them with information and insight that will be helpful as they try to understand how to help those who are suffering.

RETRIBUTIVE SUFFERING

Unquestionably, the most prominent explanation for suffering in the Bible is the principle of retribution, that is, *to give back in exact measure for what was done.* The Bible begins with the assertion of a sovereign and righteous God and teaches that prosperity is the reward for the righteous and suffering is the penalty for the unrighteous. God's activity in judging sin and rewarding obedience is clearly observable in the Old Testament.

> Then the Lord saw that the wickedness of man
> was great on the earth, and that every intent of
> the thoughts of his heart was only evil continually
> . . . . And the Lord said, "I will blot out man whom
> I have created from the face of the land . . . ; for
> I am sorry that I have made them" (Genesis 6:5-
> 7; cf. 6-8; 19; Exodus 7-12, 32 NASB).

This "retributive principle" also lay at the heart of the so-called "lament Psalms" in which the psalmists cried out to God to vindicate them. This vindication would be seen in God rewarding the psalmists and judging their prospering opponents. "Mark the blameless man, and behold the upright; For the man of peace will have a posterity. But transgressors will be altogether destroyed; The posterity of the wicked will be cut off" (Psalm 37:37-38 NASB).

This principle is also found in the prophets who proclaim imminent disaster upon the ungodly nations, as well as Israel and Judah: "Say to the righteous that it will go well with them, For they will eat the fruit of their actions. Woe to the wicked! It will go badly with him, For what he deserves will be done to him" (Isaiah 3:10-11 NASB).

While it is clear to understand that God punishes those who have evil in their hearts, those who reject him and therefore deserve his wrath, this explanation does not help when we witness innocent children suffering at the hands of evil persons. What have these innocent people done to "deserve" this retribution? Our hearts wish to say this is "not fair" and we question again, "Why does God let this happen?" This question leads us, then, to another explanation for suffering, namely, provocative suffering.

PROVOCATIVE SUFFERING

Provocative suffering is the biblical explanation of righteous suffering as that which *provokes* divine vengeance. With God as their kinsman redeemer, the righteous or socially vulnerable—such as widows, orphans, innocent children or the poor—patiently suffer injustice, knowing that their innocent suffering will provoke God to act on their behalf. We can see this principle in the following passage:

> Rejoice, O nations, with His people; For He will avenge the blood of His servants, And will render vengeance on His adversaries, And will atone for His land and His people. (Deuteronomy 32:43 NASB).

This notion is often found in the Old Testament. God responds to the cry of the victim's innocent blood by punishing the murderer or the tribe of the murderer (Genesis 4:8; 2 Kings 9:7, 2; Chronicles 24:22; Ezekiel 34:6; Psalm 9:11-12; 79:10). God also was provoked to act on a massive scale in

231

response to social oppression or widespread persecution. For example, it was the oppression of the innocent that provoked the judgment of God upon Sodom and Gomorrah:

> Then the Lord said, "The outcry against Sodom and Gomorrah is so great and their sin so grievous that I will go down and see if what they have done is as bad as the outcry that has reached me. If not, I will know" (Genesis 18:20-21; cf. Exodus 22:22-23).

This perspective is also reflected in Ezekiel's condemnation of Israel:

> "Now this was the sin of your sister Sodom:
> She and her daughters were arrogant, overfed
> and unconcerned; they did not help the poor and
> needy. They were haughty and did detestable
> things before me. Therefore I did away with them
> as you have seen" (Ezekiel 16:49-50).

Prophetic warnings continually compare Israel to Sodom and Gomorrah and the destruction of Jerusalem; the exile is at least partially explained by the cry of innocent blood which incites Yahweh's anger and forces him to act. Amos warns that God will indeed act, especially on behalf of those suffering:

> This is what the Lord says: "For three sins of
> Israel, even for four, I will not turn back my wrath.
> They sell the righteous for silver, and the needy
> for a pair of sandals. They trample on the heads
> of the poor as upon the dust of the ground and
> deny justice to the oppressed" (Amos 2:6-7).

In this passage we can see that the suffering of the righteous is actually happening in cooperation with God and the suffering helps hasten the coming of the Messianic kingdom. This suffering, then, becomes the catalyst for the cataclysmic intervention of God. In The Book of Revelation, for example, attention has been drawn to the author's unshakable belief that the innocent death of the faithful will usher in the final day of judgment (Revelation 6:9-11; 16:4-7; 18:20-24; 19:1-3). Thus, in this interpretation of righteous suffering, it is believed that God, as kinsman redeemer, protects and avenges the innocent and vulnerable. God does not always react to the crime itself but rather to the complaints, cries, prayers and even the blood of the oppressed. Indeed, the implication is that often God becomes aware of the injustice only through the testimony of the innocent.

> Do not take advantage of a widow or an orphan. If you do and they cry out to me, I will certainly hear their cry. My anger will be aroused, and I will kill you with the sword; . . . (Exodus 22:22-24).

DISCIPLINARY SUFFERING

Loving parents will discipline their children. God as our loving parent often disciplines us. This kind of suffering is not seen as punishment but as divine discipline. When God's children are disobedient they will be disciplined by God for the express purpose of bringing them back into obedience and into a close relationship with him. We can see this idea explained clearly in Proverbs 3:11-12 (NASB):

> My son, do not reject the discipline of the Lord;
> Or loathe His reproof, For whom the Lord loves
> He reproves, Even as a father the son in whom
> He delights.

This type of suffering can be seen as educational, for it is a teaching tool that instructs lessons and frames qualities essential to the "child."

A second form of disciplinary suffering is related to the first but slightly different. This form of discipline suggests that God tests his subjects (or a community) through suffering to bring out their true disposition. The suffering will then bring to the surface that which lies deep within one's heart, and one's faithfulness or unfaithfulness becomes evident. This suggestion is offered in the prologue of Job (Job 1:6-12). It is also considered the purpose of the wilderness wanderings: "In the wilderness He fed you manna which your fathers did not know, that He might humble you and that He might test you, to do good for you in the end" (Deuteronomy 8:16 NASB).

The test, therefore, provides an opportunity for God to observe that which was in the individual's heart as it emerges in external behavior.

Thirdly, disciplinary suffering is viewed as a purging or purification of the individual or the community. This belief can be detected in the image of smelting (to melt so as to separate impurities from pure metal) and refining found in the Old Testament: "I will also turn My hand against you, And will smelt away your dross as with lye, And will remove all your alloy" (Isaiah 1:25 NASB).

The disciplinary view is, in a sense, a reframe of the retributive view. Instead of being a mark of divine punishment, suffering is seen as a sign of God's loving concern. But it is his children whom God disciplines, tests and purifies. God loves his children so much that he is unable to stand by and see them destroyed by sin. God takes almost immediate action to discipline the ones whom he loves to spare them from almost certain misery.

MERITORIOUS SUFFERING

Another biblical perspective on suffering that originated in the Old Testament and developed in the New Testament was the idea of suffering as the road to future glory or exaltation. The emphasis in this interpretation stresses the fact that the sufferer is assured a glorious outcome from the present ordeal. The suffering now, that is, humiliation, will doubtless lead to glory later, or exaltation. This explanation is merely a variation of the retributive perspective; *in eternity* the righteous will be rewarded and the unrighteous will be punished.

This suffering-leads-to-glory idea has its foundation in the Old Testament especially in the wisdom literature. The earliest example is Joseph whose sale into slavery by his brothers (suffering) paved the way for his appointment by Pharaoh as second-in-command. As a result of Joseph's suffering, he was not only able to save his family from starvation but also to receive homage from them (glory). The wisdom stories incorporated into Esther and Daniel also exhibit this suffering-leads-to-glory theme. In these stories the ordeal of trial, suffering and possible martyrdom is viewed as the road the righteous must travel to gain exaltation and glory. The reward may take the form of future blessing in this life, blessing for the sufferer's descendants, blessing in eternity or even an eternal reputation (Job 42:10-17; Psalm 37).

This explanation helps solve the problem of innocent suffering by asserting that the scales of justice will be balanced *after* death when the righteous are exalted and glorified and the wicked are punished and humiliated. Therefore, suffering now is a small price to pay for the glory that is sure to follow.

REVELATIONAL SUFFERING

Yet another understanding of suffering is called by some "revelational." Revelational suffering means that as a result of their personal suffering, people can gain a deeper relational knowledge of God. God reveals himself more fully in the midst of suffering. In this deep personal suffering God's presence can be felt most intimately. Hosea's relationship with his adulterous wife, Gomer, is a good Old Testament example. The prophets of the Bible also experienced similar revelational suffering. They viewed suffering merely as an occupational hazard. It was just part and parcel of the prophet's calling.

This notion of revelational, prophetic suffering is perhaps best illustrated by the life of the prophet, Jeremiah. Jeremiah experienced a great deal of suffering, physical as well as spiritual. His suffering came as the result of his prophetic witness. But Jeremiah's suffering actually intensified his relationship with God. This idea of "revelational suffering" developed further and became an important part of the pious believer's personal faith as is observable in many of the Psalms. Thus, the righteous person who remained faithful to God and took a prophetic stance against sin and evil could only expect suffering as the direct consequence of this lifestyle. But most importantly, the prophet's innocent suffering would serve to bring him closer to God.

DEMONIC SUFFERING

Demonic activity is another interpretation found in the Scriptures for righteous suffering. The supreme example is, of course, Job who suffered as a direct result of Satan's attack (Job 1, 2). In the Old Testament, Satan, or perhaps one of his emissaries, troubles King Saul (1 Samuel 16:14-16, 23; 18:10; 19:9). The demonic character of suffering develops considerably in Daniel. Under the persecution of Antiochus, the malevolent king is portrayed as demonic in his blasphemies, arrogance and maliciousness (Daniel 7:25). The king is no less than the embodiment of Satan. In the Book of Revelation, the present persecution is also explained as a demonic rebellion, not as the divine will. But even if the suffering is a result of demonic activity, the believer can still take heart that these activities are not taking God by surprise. As in Job's situation, even the demonic activity is *totally* under God's control and will ultimately have a positive result in the life of the believer. Though Satan means it for evil, God uses it for the believer's good.

END-TIME SUFFERING

The "Day of the Lord" is a frequent theme in the Scriptures, and it is often associated with the end-time wrath of God. God's anger on that day will be so fierce that it will affect even the natural world which will be thrown into cosmic convulsions. Supernatural signs, therefore, accompany this awesome end-time event. This cataclysmic upheaval means suffering for all humankind. Chapter thirteen of Isaiah is a characteristic example:

> Wail, for the day of the Lord is near!
> It will come as destruction from the Almighty . . . .
> And every man's heart will melt.
> And they will be terrified,
> Pains and anguish will take hold of them;
> They will writhe like a woman in labor, ...
> Behold, the day of the Lord is coming,
> Cruel, with fury and burning anger, ...
> For the stars of heaven and their constellations
> Will not flash forth their light;
> The sun will be dark when it rises,
> And the moon will not shed its light.
> (Isaiah 13:6-10 NASB).

Furthermore the Book of Revelation speaks of a final period of suffering which would be far worse than any previously experienced. God has decreed a period of tribulation which will precede and signal the nearness of the coming kingdom. Thus, the intensity of the suffering serves as an instrument which measures the nearness of the kingdom and therefore the nearness of the deliverance from the suffering. The night is darkest just before the dawn.

Frequently, Israel's prophets preached that the ushering in of the kingdom would be preceded by a time of unprecedented suffering and by the domination of evil. For the righteous this meant bitter persecution; for the world at large it meant widespread disaster and all the agony that human tyranny can bring. This suffering is sometimes explained as a test sent to purify the righteous and, at other times, it is interpreted as the price paid for the glory which will surely follow. Most often, however, it is simply left unexplained; it was merely part of the predetermined program of God.

However, during horrible periods of suffering those enduring it are often in so much pain they need reassurance that history is not raging out of control. Therefore, at times it may be helpful to view suffering as related to the predestined plan of God which helps usher in the kingdom. Thus, we can be assured that God is still in control. For those in pain to see their suffering as foreordained by God may render their distress a little more bearable.

REDEMPTIVE SUFFERING

An important explanation of suffering is what can be called "redemptive" suffering. Clearly the death of Christ is sufficient to provide atonement for all believers (Mark 10:45; 2 Corinthians 5:21; Matthew 26:26-29; Mark 14:22-25; Luke 22:17-20; 1 Corinthians 11:23-25; Romans 3:25) and therefore Jesus' death is redemptive on our behalf and is all anyone needs to be saved. The question arises, however, can human suffering ever be "redemptive." A great tradition in other religions concerns the redemptive effects of human suffering. Even in late Judaism some personal suffering was considered redemptive. For example, the deaths of the martyrs in the Maccabean literature, which was written during the intertestamental period, are considered to be atoning sacrifices (2 Maccabees 7:37-38; 4 Maccabees 6:26-29; et al.). Within the biblical tradition, however, the concept of redemptive suffering is not so clear.

Redemptive suffering is central in the Servant Songs of Isaiah. In these songs the Servant voluntarily accepts suffering as the consequence for human sin, though the Servant

238

himself is innocent: "He had done no violence, nor was there any deceit found in his mouth" (Isaiah 53:9). The Servant suffers entirely on behalf of others: "He was pierced for *our* transgressions, he was crushed for *our* iniquities; the punishment that brought *us* peace was upon him, and by his wounds *we* are healed" (Isaiah 53:5 emphasis added). This is perhaps the supreme contribution of Israel's theologians to the discussion in the ancient literature which discusses innocent suffering: it may be redemptive. However, the identity of this Servant is a problem. Is the Servant a person or is the Servant the nation of Israel taken as a collective whole? Although the Servant undeniably possesses some collective characteristics and is even identified as the nation of Israel (Isaiah 49:3), any interpretation that identifies the Servant *only* in collective terms appears to have nearly insurmountable difficulties, especially when the Servant dies and comes back to life (Isaiah 53:10-12).

From this discussion it seems necessary, first, to avoid exclusive interpretations of the Servant and, second, to attribute both collective *and* individual traits to Isaiah's Servant image. The mission of the Servant of Isaiah finds its individual fulfillment in the atoning work of Christ on the cross. This much is very clear. A number of quotes and allusions link Christ's atoning work to the mission of the Servant (Mark 10:45; Matthew 26:26-29; Mark 14:22-25; Luke 22:17-20; 1 Corinthians 11:23-25). Yet what about the collective interpretation? Do the people of God also suffer redemptively? Colossians 1:22-25 sheds some light on this idea:

> But now he has reconciled you by Christ's physical body through death to present you holy in his sight, without blemish and free from accusation—if you continue in your faith, not moved from the hope held out in the gospel. This is the gospel that you heard and that has been proclaimed to every creature under heaven, and of which I, Paul, have become a servant.

239

What does Paul mean by these verses? It is difficult to conceive of something "lacking in the atoning work of Christ." Notice here that the passage is framed with the word *servant*, which in the context of suffering, especially Christ's suffering, is almost certainly an allusion to the Servant of Isaiah. It seems that for Paul the collective sense of the ministry of the Servant is in view so that he can understand his suffering as part of the Servant's suffering. This idea does not mean that Paul's suffering is atoning, but it is part of the Servant's ministry. In Isaiah 52:13 the Servant causes many (even kings) to be astonished.

The ministry of the Servant, as the Servant suffers, is a compelling sight and gives pause to those watching the Servant. This dimension of the ministry of the Servant is probably the one Paul is fastening upon in his Colossians passage. This part of the Servant's ministry has collective dimensions and "fills up what was lacking in the suffering of Christ." In other words as the people of God suffer and experience the strength that God supplies, their responses are seen by the watching world as winsome and attractive. Their gracious witness draws others to Christ.

In this way the suffering of the people of God is redemptive, though not atoning. In this way the people of God "fill up what was lacking in the sufferings of Christ" and help fulfill the ministry of the Suffering Servant. When helping believers make some sense out of their own personal pain, we can perhaps help them to hold on to the concept that, somehow, the way in which they graciously respond to suffering may actually lead others to a saving knowledge of Jesus Christ.

ENIGMATIC SUFFERING

Finally, some righteous suffering exists in Scripture that is ultimately incomprehensible to the human mind. From time to time in biblical literature the writer concludes that some suffering just does not make any sense. To Habakkuk and Job, for example, suffering just seems to be a mystery of God's doing what our minds and hearts cannot penetrate.

Agonizing over unpunished sin, innocent suffering and injustice in his land, Habakkuk finally leaves the problem unsolved and cries out to God:

> How long, O Lord, must I call for help, but you do not listen? Or cry out to you, "Violence!" but you do not save? Why do you make me look at injustice? Why do you tolerate wrong? . . . The wicked hem in the righteous, so that justice is perverted (Habakkuk 1:2-4).

God answers that he is gathering the Chaldean army to come and punish the Israelites (1:5–11). But instead of finding relief with this answer, Habakkuk is appalled and in the next paragraph (1:12–17) he challenges God's logic and the morality of his answer. Since Babylonia is more wicked than Israel, how can that nation be the executor of justice? The reply from God is direct, "the righteous will live by his faith" (2:4). In other words, "Trust me, I know what I'm doing." This explanation is final for Habakkuk.

So also in Job, the reason for suffering is enigmatic. In the opening scene of this drama, the poet is swift to note that the victim is innocent: "He is blameless and upright, a man who fears God and shuns evil" (Job 1:8). Throughout the rest of the book Job defends his innocence in the face of his three friends' accusations. His friends argue that no one is completely innocent, and even the most righteous of all has a long list of sins committed unwittingly.

But Job knows that his suffering is disproportionate to any sins he knowingly or unknowingly may have committed. Job, therefore, after reaching the point of utter despair, cries out to God and demands an explanation. God then appears in a tempest and gives Job an answer, explaining to Job that his own individual problem must be seen in the greater context of creation as a whole. The problem for Job, however, is that he does not have the ability to comprehend the whole. Any one individual is such a tiny part of God's overall plan that, without the big picture, a person cannot possibly understand what

God is doing. So Job ends in the same place as Habakkuk: trust God and believe that ultimately it does make sense.

Thus, the answer for the book of Job is that some suffering must, in the final analysis, remain unexplained because the ways of God are too exalted for humankind to understand. Since God's wisdom is beyond the human understanding, suffering, especially righteous suffering, for both Job and Habakkuk, ultimately remains a mystery.

SUMMARY

So then, when we ask and are asked the questions "Where is God in this suffering?" "Why does God allow the innocent to suffer?" "Can we find God in the midst of this horror?" It seems important to look at the insightful, biblical explanations of suffering and try to present God as "in" the suffering. He is "in" the suffering redemptively and revelationally. We can call out to him and feel his unique presence in the midst of the horror. We can even take heart that perhaps God will bring others to himself because of the suffering, and that this present situation is not taking God by surprise. He has all things under his control for the purpose of his plan, which is much more comprehensive than ours.

As we have looked into some explanations for suffering, we have found a number of complementary interpretations. It must be remembered to take these perspectives holistically, because they all overlap. Originally they were carefully woven into a single garment— Israel trying to make sense of the suffering they were experiencing as a nation and as individuals. Multiple interpretations could exist around the same event. These explanations are not all mutually exclusive. Clearly the Scriptures work hard to explain this difficult notion of suffering, especially innocent suffering. May we in our generation work equally hard at applying the biblical material to our own situations and help bring understanding and, ultimately, trust in God to those who suffer.

Part 5

Concluding Reflections

Part 3

Concluding Reflections

21

A New Commitment

Larry W. Sharp

One must assume that a book with a title such as *Children in Crisis: A New Commitment* demands change on the part of the readers. Something new and different should take place within the hearts and lives of thinking, caring Christians, within our churches and within our mission institutions.

We certainly must have been overwhelmed and stunned by references to a "globally endemic outrage," of children being "sold into prostitution," "children's tragic plight," children "at phenomenal risk" and "painful childhoods." The endemic nature of the problem has been described with a plethora of statistics, and true stories have sobbed out the reality of children in crisis. In summary, the data remind us that nearly one-half of the world's people are children. The majority of them are suffering, most live in the Two-Thirds world and 80 percent grow up in non-Christian settings.

Thus, with a clear cognitive recognition of the need, along with a reminder of the biblical mandate and even some great examples and ideas of what is being done by a few, what more is needed? Where do we go from here? What is lacking? The missing link must certainly be in us. The internalization of these realities within our own hearts and beings must move us to act.

The essays of this book convey the design of God for restoring "childhood" to children victimized by the tragic plight of a sin-driven world. However, the achievement of God's compassion-driven purposes rest with another segment of this fallen world—committed Christians who understand and take seriously God's call to commitment.

Individuals, churches and mission agencies have not always been remiss in responding to the challenge of children. Monsma correctly observes that ministry to children is not a novel idea in the history of missions. That the children of today's world do not line up conveniently in school desks and are not easily gathered into church pews creates the novelty. The sociological realities demand new and creative methodologies. They demand Christian commitment of a different sort. Clearly, children cannot be ignored in global, regional and local church-planting strategies. In fact, they should be at the core of such efforts. Humans of all ages must be targeted and embraced. With so many children on the periphery of society and affluence, both creative, energetic strategies and total commitment will be required to meet their needs.

Woods and Levinson remind us that society can successfully combine creative energy with total commitment. The example of the efforts to save the world's whales is a penetrating illustration of what can be done when humankind decides to rise to a challenge. Can the body of Christ do less?

Sociologists suggest that the term "commitment" is used to explain consistent behavior. When a person links all areas of life together with a consistent line of activity to which he or she is pledged, that person is committed. As Christians seek "a new commitment" to the challenges of the world's children, perhaps we need to keep three things in mind. First, a commitment is rooted in the essence of our Savior's example and our prayerful communion with him today. Second, we need to realize we can't turn around the plight of 1.8 billion children ourselves, but we can start somewhere to do something. Third, we should not be discouraged: ministering to children is really worth it!

246

JESUS' EXAMPLE FOR TODAY'S REALITIES

To be committed is to line up our behavior in a consistent manner with our beliefs. We believe the Bible; we believe the truth of Jesus' teachings; we believe we should practice what we preach. As we approach the end of this century and endeavor to save the world's children, we must ask ourselves, what *did* Jesus do? What *would* Jesus do? What should *we* do?

We can be confident that Jesus would do what he did two thousand years ago, as reported in Matthew 18. He said he is "not willing that any of these little ones should be lost." He said that adult-driven people like the disciples should "see that you do not look down on one of these little ones." As if that was not challenge enough, he continued, "unless you change and become like little children, you will never enter the kingdom of heaven," and "whoever welcomes a little child like this in my name welcomes me."

Jesus' perspective grows even more intense. Greatness in heaven is a correlate with the humility of a little child, and judgment awaits "anyone who causes one of these little ones who believe in me to sin"—severe punishment indeed! Our commitment may then be motivated by a desire for greatness or by a fear of judgment. Whatever the source of our commitment to a consistent application of Jesus' teachings, such application certainly will be demonstrated in the life of a child. Children are important—to Jesus, intrinsically important—and important to the church.

What would Jesus do? He would seek, care for, love, welcome, elevate and enjoy children. Can we do less?

Jesus sets this all in perspective in Luke 10 when, shortly after Luke's parallel account of how children are of great importance, he relates to his disciples that "the harvest is plentiful, but the workers are few. Ask the Lord of the harvest, therefore, to send out workers into his harvest field."

Jesus says that children are important, and they are part of the harvest. Harvesters are needed. We can pray about that.

Will you pray? The genius of prayer is that it is communion with God. If we are listening, we may hear clues on how to be part of a compassionate response to the needs of children. Prayer may be a new commitment to children in crisis.

START SMALL, NOW, HERE

No one of us can turn the children's dilemma around; not even one church denomination or one mission agency can do it. We are in this commitment together, and we will all need to do our part. Begin small, doing something, somewhere, somehow—NOW!

Start in the most basic of all institutions, the family. If *our* marriages and *our* families are safe, happy places where people are loved and secure, the stage will be set for our children to care for others. However, too many Christian families are embroiled in tensions arising from a mother and father who neither demonstrate unconditional love for each other nor for their children. No wonder God's purposes for the children of the world are not understood and realized!

What better place than the family to educate children to a practical involvement in missions? Steps can be taken to help children learn about a "world" of difference. Our children can learn that the God of the universe is not for them only but also for others around the world who are very different. Our kids can make a difference if we hold them to right challenges and realistic visions.

The Kids Can Make a Difference program promotes the idea that children are not just an "end" or "object" of ministry. They can become involved in outreach, care giving, missions trips, financial giving and prayer. By starting with children in our families and churches, we can develop a generation that will rise to the challenge and make a difference.

Churches that have learned the secret of involving Baby Boomers and Generation Xers in missions have discovered that learning is best effected when implemented in small steps. Why not set up a six- or eight-step process beginning with one evening or one class or one visit with a missionary committed to children's ministries? The next step could be a weekend retreat or a multi-lesson class or seminar followed by a visit to an inner-city street-children's work. Gradually, over some months, a compassionate conviction will emerge and demonstrate a commitment to children in crisis through personal involvement, giving or diligent targeted prayer. A good many will go overseas, devoting time, energy, skill and finances to make a difference in the lives of other children.

Start small but do something! Ask others for ideas before you try to reinvent the wheel. Check out some of the Tool Box ideas in the appendix of this book. Take small steps with a few interested friends or children. Jesus started with one child; he "took a little child. . . and said to [his disciples], 'Whoever welcomes this little child in my name welcomes me'" (Luke 9:46, 48).

COMMITMENT WORTH THE SACRIFICE

We have every reason to be encouraged; devoting our energies and resources to nearly one-half of the world's people is of great value. Naturally, these children will outlive the rest of us and continue to affect the world. Some studies indicate that as many as 85 percent of all people who come to Christ, do so between the ages of four and fourteen. When Christ changes children, the vital difference made in their lives is our encouragement.

I came to realize the full impact of the effects of a targeted youth program for adolescents some years ago while serving as the Brazil field director for UFM International. I got to know many pastors of churches in the north and northeast of Brazil. As we talked together, time after time they gave credit to the Jet Cadet youth program of the national church, started more than 25 years ago to provide for the youth of the church. The dedicated work of foreign missionaries and national workers, as well as the prayers and finances from hundreds of people, have provided for this program in more than 100 churches.

Many of the pastors told me they are following God today and made it through the difficult teen years in Brazil because of this program in their churches. Here is one program with many committed workers and with definable results. Clearly, this program is "worth it!"

Not long ago, two other missionaries and I boarded a bus just before midnight in the heart of the world's third-largest city, Sao Paulo, Brazil. Perhaps nothing affected me more deeply that night than the story of Leonardo.

John, my missionary colleague, said to me, "Do you see that young fellow who followed us onto the bus?" Leonardo and his three friends looked sharp and easily could have passed for friends of my own teenage sons. Leonardo, at 18 years, was a testimony to what the gospel, along with the tireless efforts of street workers, can do in Sao Paulo.

John found Leonardo at age 12 on a city street. There the boy cared for five younger siblings while his mother worked as a prostitute in the sleaziest section of Sao Paulo's "Mouth of Garbage" district. Night after night and year after year Leonardo cared for his suffering family—no father, no change, no hope.

John was able to bring a little relief to these suffering souls and enrolled Leonardo in a scout program for street boys. Before long Leonardo came to know Christ. Thus began the long road to restructuring Leonardo's values and those of his mother and siblings. That road continues today, but Leonardo is progressing in school, has brought other street boys to the Savior and is working to provide for his family.

Tears flooded my eyes as my emotions processed the knowledge of all the abuse, sin, filth, immorality, poverty and dysfunction which Leonardo had experienced. I realized what commitment it took for John and his wife to come and live in that pit of hell to reach out to children like Leonardo. What joy to see the changes so evident that night. Seeking lost children is worth it! Real changes do occur, and lives are different because people care about kids.

WHAT I SHOULD AND CAN DO, I WILL DO

What children need most is to know that God loves them, forgives their sins and accepts them as his children. The love of God is shown clearly when committed Christians with compassion give time, skill, protection, care, respect and love. In this way, God's power is unleashed and a world is changed.

For the church, for mission agencies and for anyone committed to the church as a primary institution for the unity of Christians, children must be an integral part of all strategies. Jesus was not adult-driven only. He was people-driven. Our ministries and outreaches must holistically encompass humanity, both young and old.

> I am only one, but I am one.
> I cannot do everything, but I can do something;
> and what I should do and can do, I will do.

Appendix

TOOL BOX SAMPLER
Resource Agencies and Materials

I. Children-focused Mission Organizations

Action International

Mr. Doug Nichols, International Director
Mr. Marvin Graves, U. S. Director
P.O. Box 490
Bothell, WA 98041-0490
Telephone: 206-485-1967

Focus: Engaged in evangelism among street children and the urban poor.

Programs: Camping, church planting and leadership development.

Countries Served: Brazil, Colombia, India, Mexico and Philippines.

Communiqué: *Street Children Letter* (quarterly).

The Arms of Jesus Children's Mission, Inc.

Dr. Sam Martin, Director
Suite 160, Unit 9, 1848 Liverpool Road
Pickering, Ontario, L1V 6M3 Canada
Telephone: 905-509-6140
Fax: 905-509-6141

Focus: Street children, orphans, children in poverty.

Programs: Medical ministries, sponsorship programs, education and feeding centers.

Countries Served: Haiti, Guatemala, the Dominican Republic, Kenya, Uganda, Zaire, Thailand.

Communiqué: Published report (three-four times yearly).

Child Evangelism Fellowship, Inc.

Mr. Reese R. Kauffman, President
P.O. Box 348
Warrenton, MO 63383-0348
Telephone: 314-456-4321
Fax: 314-456-2078

CHILD EVANGELISM FELLOWSHIP™ INC.

Focus: To evangelize boys and girls with the gospel of the Lord Jesus Christ and to establish (disciple) them in the Word of God and in a local church for Christian living.

Programs: Engaged in evangelism through Good News Clubs, 5-day Clubs, Tel-a-story ministry (telephone), fairs and camping programs.

Countries Served: CEF has developed work in 132 countries in Africa, Asia, Canada, Latin America, the Middle East, Oceana and in all the U.S.A. states.

Communiqué: *Evangelizing Today's Child* (bimonthly).

Dorcas Aid International

Mr. Ken Sweers, Chief Executive Officer
6475 28th Street S.E., Suite 233
Grand Rapids, MI 49546
Phone: 616-363-5860
Fax: 616-454-3456

DORCAS AID INTERNATIONAL

Focus: Christian relief and development through national workers.

Programs: Street children programs, camps, schools, hospitals and orphanages.

Countries Served: 26 countries in Africa, Eastern Europe, Mid-East and New Independent States (NIS).

Communiqué: *Dorcas Journal* (quarterly).

Freedom In Christ Ministries

Dr. Neil T. Anderson, President
491 E. Lambert Road
La Habra, CA 90631
Telephone: 310-691-9128
Fax: 310-691-4035

Friends in the West

Mr. Raymond R. Barnett, President
P. O. Box 250
Arlington, WA 98223
Phone: 206-435-8983
Fax: 206-435-6334

Programs: Child care, camping, community development, literacy work and relief aid. Also sponsors the African Children's Choir. The purpose of the children's choir is to help create new leadership for tomorrow's Africa.

Countries Served: Kenya, Lebanon, Romania, Uganda, Rwanda.

Communiqué: *Between Friends* (quarterly).

Hearts of the Father Outreach

John and Libby Moritz, Directors and Founders
P.O. Box 491
Undermountain Road
Sheffield, MA 01257
Telephone: 413-229-2922
Fax: 413-229-3257

Focus: To establish homes of refuge for orphaned, abandoned and abused children, safe harbors for those caught in the unexpected storms of life; help existing ministries to children.

Programs: Through the homes to provide love, nurturing, educational and vocational training.

Countries Served: Mexico, Guatemala, Ghana, Grenada.

Communiqué: Quarterly four-page newsletter.

Homeless Children International

Homeless Children International, Inc.
David M. High, President
P. O. Box 53026
Knoxville, TN 37950
Telephone: 423-691-5048

Focus: Sharing Christ and providing shelter for abandoned children living on the streets of the world.

Programs: Home construction, sports clubs for street children, feeding programs, vocational training, educational training, emergency aid and drug rehabilitation.

Countries Served: Bolivia, Brazil, Kenya and Peru.

Communiqué: Bi-monthly prayer letter and semi-annual newsletter, *Realize.*

KIDS ALIVE!

Kids Alive International
John M. Rock, President
2507 Cumberland Drive
Valparaiso, IN 46383
Telephone: 219-464-9035
Fax: 219-462-5611

Focus: Disadvantaged homeless children overseas whose families are unwilling or unable to care for them. This includes abandoned and street children, orphans, children with only one parent who is financially unable to care for them and children from dysfunctional or abusive families. Some of these children are the victims of local hostilities. All of the children come from poverty-stricken backgrounds.

Programs: Primarily residential Children's Homes, schools and day programs. The children usually enter a Home at about age 4 and stay until they graduate from high school at age 18.

Countries Served: Pacific Rim - Taiwan, Papua New Guinea.
Middle East - Lebanon.
Latin America - Dominican Republic, Mexico, Guatemala, Peru.

Communiqué: *The Harvester* newsletter.

Kids Can Make A Difference

Jan Bell, Founder
4445 Webster Drive
York, PA 17402
Telephone: 717-757-6793
Fax: 717-757-6103

Focus: Giving children a missions vision.

Program: Equipping adults who work with children through workshops, networking and resource catalog.

Countries Served: Primarily North America, expanding internationally.

Communiqué: KidsCan Network Catalog; kids-can-net, an on-line network for sharing ideas and resources.

Oakseed

Oakseed Ministries International
Ed Bradley, President
P. O. Box 11222
Burke, VA 22009
Telephone: 703-455-2652
Fax: 703-455-3904

Focus: To help abandoned children, the poor and society's castoffs through mentoring, consulting, training, ministry formation, restoration and proclamation. Not a sending mission, Oakseed forms partnerships with indigenous missions and seeks to facilitate partner relationships between local churches and indigenous missions.

Programs: Schools, orphanages, child sponsorship, drug rehabilitation and programs for prisoners, street children, widows and prostitutes.

Countries Served: Focuses on megacities in Latin America, Africa, Eastern Europe and Asia.

Communiqué: A quarterly church bulletin insert, *Cry of the City*, in both adult and children's edition.

Youth with a Mission

Mr. Loren Cunningham, International Director
Mr. Steve Goode, Director of
Mercy Ministries International
GPO Box 177
Bangkok 10501 Thailand

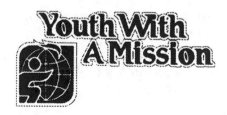

Focus: Evangelism, missionary orientation, mobilization for mission, relief aid and youth programs.

Programs: Include rehabilitation centers, street children, orphanages and relief aid.

Countries Served: Worldwide.

Communiqué: *Going Concerns* (bimonthly).

II. Networks

Alliance for Children Everywhere (ACE)

"From God's Hands…The World's Children"

Jennie Wood, President
P. O. Box 912
Bothell, WA 98041-0912
Telephone: 206-402-4065
Fax: 206-488-8316

Alliance for Children Everywhere is a network that speaks and acts on behalf of traumatized and abandoned children worldwide. ACE engages all members of society in the challenges facing the world's children. Partnering with churches, agencies, businesses and mission groups ensures optimum use of resources. They have developed curriculum for youth's involvement in the mission task. (Check the curriculum section.)

Esther Network International: Children's Global Prayer Movement

Esther Ilnisky, Founder and Director
854 Conniston Road
West Palm Beach, FL 33405-2131
Telephone: 407-832-6490
Fax: 407-932-8043

Vision: to mobilize and network a global "army" of praying children – MILLIONS STRONG – united to reach their generation.

Purpose: to teach, train, equip children and leaders so that children can be praying "world shapers."

Motto: "CATCH THE VISION – GET GLOBAL."

KIDS-CAN-NET

The purpose of kids-can-net is to facilitate networking among those interested in giving the next generation a missions vision. The distinctives of kids-can-net relating to missions education include: understanding "kid culture," learning about children in difficult situations, developing a world view perspective, equipping children for ministry and integrating missions in curriculum using the framework of the "P" words (see curriculum). The on-line network is free. To subscribe, send a message to HUB@XC.org "Subscribe kids-can-net" "youremailaddress" (without quotes).

The Viva Network

Mr. Patrick McDonald,
International Coordinator
ICO: P.O. Box 633
Oxford, OX2 ONS
England
Fax: 44-865-727-421

The Viva Network seeks to serve those already engaged in meeting the needs of children at high social risk, and to support emerging projects in every way possible. The network seeks to be an international vehicle of joint actions, cooperation and exchange of ideas and information for all Christians involved in ministry to children at social risk.

Communiqué: *Children at Risk Prayer Diary* (bimonthly).

III. Relief and Development

Compassion International, Inc.

Dr. Wesley K. Stafford, President
P. O. Box 7000
Colorado Springs, CO 80918
Fax: 719-594-6271

Compassion International is an evangelical child development ministry dedicated to addressing the needs of children in Africa, Central America, South America, Asia, and North America. More than a relief program, Compassion focuses on the real life needs of children — spiritual, physical, economic and social.

Communiqué: *Compassion Update* (bimonthly).

Samaritan's Purse

Rev. W. Franklin Graham, President
P.O. Box 3000
Boone, NC 28607
Fax: 704-262-1796

A nondenominational service agency of evangelical tradition engaged in relief aid, agricultural programs, evangelism, funds transmission, support of national workers and supplying equipment.

Communiqué: *Samaritan's Purse Newsletter* (monthly).

World Vision

Dr. Robert A. Seiple, President
P.O. Box 9716
Federal Way, WA 98063-9716
Fax: 206-815-3140

An interdenominational service agency of evangelical tradition engaged in child care programs, community development, relief aid, evangelism, leadership development and medical work.

Communiqué: *World Vision* (bimonthly); *Childlife* (quarterly); *Partners* (quarterly).

IV. Books

Anderson, Jeff; *Crisis on the Streets: A Manual for Ministry to Street Children*, published by ACTION Publishing and Urban Street Ministries, the Republic of the Philippines.

Anderson, Neil T. and Russo, Steve; *The Seduction of Our Children* (Protecting Kids From Satanism, New Age and the Occult); Harvest House Publishers.

Other books by Neil T. Anderson include:
Victory Over the Darkness
The Bondage Breaker
The Bondage Breaker Youth Edition
Stomping Out the Darkness
Helping Others Find Freedom in Christ

Aptekar, Lewis; *Street Children of Cali;* Duke University Press.

Bascom, Dr. Barb and McKelvey, Carole A.; *Through the Golden Doors: A Primer on International Adoption;* Simon and Schuster, Publishers.

Blankenhorn, David; *Fatherless America: Confronting Our Most Urgent Social Problem;* Basic Books.

Brown, Fletch; *Street Boy;* The Moody Bible Institute of Chicago, available from Action International Ministries.

Butcher, Andy; *Street Children: The Tragedy and Challenge of the World's Millions of Modern-day Oliver Twists;* Nelson-Word (UK), (Spring 1996).

CEF; *Children's Ministry Resource Bible;* Thomas Nelson Publishers. Contains teacher training aids, Bible lesson outlines, full-page articles and much more.

Dallape, Fabio; *An Experience with Street Children*; Undugu Society, P.O. Box 40417, Nairobi, Kenya.

Dimenstein, Gilberto; *Brazil: War on Children;* Latin American Bureau.

Garland, Diana; *Precious in His Sight: A Guide to Child Advocacy;* New Hope Publishers, Birmingham, AL.

Grigg, Viv; *Companion to the Poor;* MARC, World Vision.

Grigg, Viv; *Cry of the Urban Poor;* MARC, World Vision.

Ilnisky, Esther; *What about the Children?;* Esther Network International.

Kilbourn, Phyllis, ed.; *Healing the Children of War,* a handbook for children who have suffered deep trauma; MARC, World Vision.

Kilbourn, Phyllis, ed.; *A* handbook for ministry to street children; MARC, World Vision, (Spring 1997).

Magid, Dr. Ken and McKelvey, Carole A.; *High Risk Children Without a Conscience;* Bantam Books.

Murray, Andrew; *How to Raise Your Children for Christ;* Bethany House Publishers.

Strobel, Charles F.; *Room in the Inn: Ways Your Congregation Can Help Homeless People;* Abington Press, Nashville, TN.

Tesch, Wayne & Diane; *Unlocking the Secret World.* This book will help you recognize the signs of child abuse, the profile of the abuser and then show actions to take. From: Royal Family Kids' Camps, Inc., 1068 Salinas Avenue, Costa Mesa, CA 92626.

Wilson, Bill; *Whose Child Is This?;* Metro Ministries.

Wirth, Eileen M. and Worden, Joan; *How to Adopt a Child from Another Country;* Abington Press, Nashville, TN.

Zutt, Johannes; *Children of War: Wandering Alone in Southern Sudan;* United Nations Children's Fund, 3 UN Plaza, H9F, New York, NY 10017.

V. Videos

The Wild Side; presents America's mission field in the inner city. Walk through the ghettos with Metro Ministries staff. (Metro Ministries; 1-800-462-7770)

The American Dream; documents the battles young urban Americans fight to see their dreams come true and the people who give them the courage to do it. (Metro Ministries)

Streets of Pain; a graphic account of what can happen when one is hooked on "the needle." Shot in the Bushwick neighborhood, shows close up how the lives of addicts and prostitutes end up as they tell their stories. (Metro Ministries)

Missing; evangelistic/family-viewing drama about a street boy in Manila. Available with discussion materials on church loan from Gospel Films, 2735 East Apple Avenue, Muskegon, MI 49442.

World, Meet Your Children; Alliance for Children Everywhere. Introduces the realities of the children's world of trauma and pain. Includes ideas on how to become actively involved.

Giving Children a Biblical World View Focused on God's Mission; enables you to train others. Presents Jan Bell demonstrating the "P" words to children and adults with easy-to-use teaching methods.

Child Evangelism Fellowship has three videos providing various aspects of training in child evangelism: *How to Lead a Child to Christ* (using the *Wordless Book*); *Child-Size Good News;* and *Child-Size Steps in Growing*.

Living Bridge; describes Compassion's vision and explains how they are affecting the lives of children around the world; from Compassion International, 10 minutes.

My Story; contains three different stories depicting a day in the life of a child from a developing country (Guatemala, the Philippines and Uganda); from Compassion International, 45 minutes.

VI. Curriculum and Resource Material

It's Time to Care for Children Everywhere is a program designed by the Alliance for Children Everywhere (ACE) as a powerful tool to teach youth about missions and to enable them to participate, at a relational level, in ministries to children. The program includes curriculum materials and "It's Time to Care for Children Everywhere" T-shirts to use as fundraisers.

World Week, created by photojournalist Chris Redner and now a project of ACE, includes more than fifteen fun and educational activities designed to help young people understand what life is like for people suffering from disease, discrimination, violence, hunger and environmental disasters.

The *Bridge-Builders* is a discipleship program that provides summer and weekend opportunities for youth to become involved in church mission outreach teams. The children minister through the performing arts, prayer walks and community outreach programs that focus on practical service. Contact Rev. Pete Hohmann, Mechanicsville Christian Center, 8556 Shady Grove Road, Mechanicsville, VA 23111 or telephone 804-746-4303 for more details.

Kids Can Make a Difference uses ten "P" words to provide a framework that answers the question, "What do we mean when we say the word 'missions'?" When we teach children the "P" words, they are able to see the world from God's perspective and develop the critical thinking skills needed in this complex world.

Three of the 10 "P" Words

PURPOSE	POWER	PEOPLE
	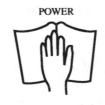	
GET THE POINT OF THE BIBLE	WHO'S GOT THE POWER?	LEARNING TO BE BRIDGE BUILDERS

Used by permission of Kids Can Make a Difference. Write to KIDSCAN at 4445 Webster Drive, York, PA 17402 for information on obtaining the complete program.

Freedom in Christ Ministries provides training material on leading people to freedom in Christ. There is a basic program and an advance course dealing with specific issues. Materials include books, study guides and tape series (both video and audio). The tape series all have corresponding syllabi. The best training occurs when trainees watch the videos, read the books and complete the study guides. Complete details are available from: Freedom in Christ Ministries, 491 E. Lambert Road, La Habra, CA 90631 (telephone: 310-691-9128; fax: 310-691-4035).

Children's Missions Resource Center

Gerry Dueck, Director
Children's Mission Resource Center
1605 Elizabeth Street
Pasadena, CA 91104
Phone: 818-398-2232

Services offered include:

- a lending library (locally)
- books, materials, brochures
- children's missionary conference packets
- assistance with planning children's missions education in the church
- craft and decorative ideas
- a regular newsletter
- provides national network listing of writers, publishers, churches and agencies.

Cry of the City is a unique activity resource for North American children to use to pray for the needs of the world's children; produced by Oakseed.

One Big House takes children (9-14 years) on an exciting journey around the world. Children will travel to a "super dump" that 20,000 people in Manila call home, to Africa for an exciting game of *Ebenga*, spears not included! From one area of the world to the next, this book takes kids on a global quantum leap through its research, engaging activities and eye-catching graphics; available from Compassion International.

You Can Change the World by Jill Johnstone contains fifty-two imaginative, full-color double-page spreads complete with maps, illustrations, information and exciting stores. This book encourages children to pray for countries and people's groups all over the world (WEC International). Use with *You Can Change the World Activity Book,* OM Publishers.

CEF: Christian Youth in Action; young people from local churches reaching children with the gospel in 5-day clubs, camps, fairs and personal witnessing; excellent training provided.

Jubilee Action, a Christian-based advocacy group taking action for the suffering church worldwide, produces *Street Life,* a complete training module on street children. *Street Life* is a superb resource for schools, youth groups and workshops containing high school level student work sheets with professionally-researched lesson plans, mini-posters, world map, photos and more. For further information contact Jubilee Action, St. John's, Cranleigh Road, Wonersh, Guildford, England GU5 OQX; fax: (01483) 894797.

VII. Catalogs

CEF Press Catalog; visualized Bible lessons, missionary stories, songs, tracts, videos and other vital aids for children's ministries. Request a free catalog.

Esther Prayer Network; a resource catalog of prayer tools including the "globall," cassette tapes, 10/40 window display for prayer, games, banners and much more.

KIDSCAN Network Catalog; 5-day VBS programs and lots of other curriculum materials, books, videos, music, creative drama. 1-800-543-7554. The catalog is also available on the KIDSCAN Network (see networks on page 10).

Metro Ministries Resource Catalog; books, videos, training materials for inner city ministry, teaching games and other curriculum tools, T-shirts. 1-800-462-7770.

VIII. Training Opportunities

CEF; Children's Ministries Institute; Specialized training in children's ministries for beginning and experienced workers. The 12-week curriculum, in its three phases, provides practical instruction for ministering directly to children, training adults to teach children and administering children's work.

CEF; Summer Urban Ministries; Practical training and experience in evangelizing and ministering to children in the inner city.

International Health Services; Disaster Relief School; an intense 9-day (12-hour/day) cross-pollinating school to prepare non-health and health-care personnel spiritually, emotionally and intellectually to respond on multi-national teams which target unreached peoples of the world. Includes wilderness survival, mock disaster, administrative planning and logistics for disasters and introduction to emergency medical care. Write to International Health Services at P.O. Box 701025, Tulsa, OK 74170 for further details.

**MARC**

Bringing you key resources on the world mission of the church

MARC books and other publications support the work of MARC (Mission Advanced Research and Communications Center), which is to inspire fresh vision and empower Christian mission among those who extend the whole gospel to the whole world.

Recent MARC titles include:

▶ *Healing the Children of War*, Phyllis Kilbourn. A practical handbook for ministry to children who have suffered deep traumas. Examines the impact of war on children; the grieving child; forgiveness; restoring hope to the child; and many other important issues that surround children who have been victimized by war. $21.95

▶ *Signs of Hope in the City*, Robert C. Linthicum. Christian leaders from around the world discuss the critical issues that will surround urban mission in the 21st century. $7.95

▶ *God So Loves the City: Seeking a Theology for Urban Mission*, Charles Van Engen and Jude Tiersma, editors. Experienced urban practitioners from around the world explore the most urgent issues facing those who minister in today's cities in search of a theology for urban mission. $21.95

▶ *By Word, Work and Wonder*, Thomas H. McAlpine. Examines the question of holism in Christian mission and brings you several case studies from around the world that will push your thinking on this important topic. $15.95

▶ *The Changing Shape of World Mission* by Bryant L. Myers. Presents in color graphs, charts and maps the challenge before global missions, including the unfinished task of world evangelization. Also available in color slides and overheads—excellent for presentations!

Book... $ 5.95
Slides.. $ 99.95
Overheads....................................... $ 99.95
Presentation Set *(one book, slides and overheads)* $175.00

Order Toll Free in USA: 1-800-777-7752
Visa and MasterCard accepted

MARC A division of World Vision International
121 E. Huntington Dr. • Monrovia • CA • 91016-3400

Ask for the MARC Newsletter and complete publications list